VANISHED ARMIES

A Record of Military Uniform
Observed and Drawn in Various
European Countries During
the Years 1908–14

A. E. HASWELL MILLER

With notes and memories of the days before
'The lights went out in Europe' in the year 1914

Edited by John Mollo

SHIRE PUBLICATIONS

First published in Great Britain in 2009 by
Shire Publications Ltd, Midland House, West Way,
Botley, Oxford OX2 0PH, United Kingdom.
44-02 23rd Street, Suite 219, Long Island City, New York, 11101, USA.
E-mail: shire@shirebooks.co.uk   www.shirebooks.co.uk

A CIP catalogue record for this book is available from the British Library.

Shire General no. 1   ·   ISBN-978 0 74780 739 1

The Army Museums Ogilby Trust has asserted its right under the Copyright, Designs and Patents Act, 1988, to be identified as the copyright holder of this book.

Edited by John Mollo

Designed by Tony Truscott Designs, Cambridge, UK and typeset in Adobe Caison Pro
Printed in China through Worldprint Ltd.

09 10 11 12 13   10 9 8 7 6 5 4 3 2 1

CONTENTS

PREFACE

This beautiful collection of paintings of military figures is by Archibald Elliott Haswell Miller, a Scottish soldier, painter and historian. He studied at the Glasgow School of Art from 1906 to 1908, becoming a probationary professor, and then travelled to study in Paris, Vienna, Munich and Berlin. The book results largely from those travels and illustrates the uniforms of British and other European armies, mainly from 1908 to 1914, reflecting a period of military elegance soon to be eclipsed by the horrors of the First World War. During that war, Haswell Miller served with the 7th (Blythswood) Battalion of the Highland Light Infantry in Gallipoli, Palestine and France. He was awarded the Military Cross, attained the rank of Captain and continued to sketch and paint as opportunities arose. He became a prolific painter of military portraits, and his work was exhibited at the Royal Academy, the Royal Scottish Academy, the Royal Institute of Oil Painters, the Royal Society of British Artists, Glasgow Institute and elsewhere.

Haswell Miller died in 1979, aged ninety-two. For the last twenty-five years of his life he was an adviser to the Army Museums Ogilby Trust. It was through this connection that the paintings came into my possession when, in 2006, his daughter sought my help in sorting through his material, some of which had been carefully stored for over seventy years. She was extremely generous in the disposal of some original works to regimental museums and expressed a strong desire that this collection of paintings and notes be published.

Colin Sibun
Director, Army Museums Ogilby Trust

EDITOR'S PREFACE

Information about the dress of the armies of Europe in the last years before 1914 can be found in numerous separate publications, but it is rare to find it all together in one book, and certainly not one illustrated with figures as colourful and lively as those reproduced here. Eyewitness information is always the most regarded, both for its artistic quality and as confirmation, or otherwise, of the regulations, soldiers being well known for having ideas of their own as to how they should dress. The beauty of this book lies in the fact that these are eyewitness sketches, the plates being reproduced from the pages the artist tore out of the sketchbooks he carried with him at the time.

Haswell Miller, as he was generally known, was, in his own words, born into a 'rather nondescript "class"' in

Glasgow, in 1887. At an early age he developed a deep interest in military uniforms and had enormous difficulty in finding out anything about them. After studying at the Glasgow School of Art, under the eminent painter Maurice Greiffenhagen, who had only just taken charge of the Life Department, he embarked in the autumn of 1908 on the first of several European tours, which lasted on and off until the outbreak of war in 1914.

It was on the first of these, in Munich, that he set about recording the soldiers he saw on the streets in a small sketchbook. From the evidence of some of the unfinished pages which are included here, and other pages of rough sketches and notes, it is clear that his method was to make a quick pencil sketch of his subject, jotting down the details and colouring of the uniform on the back or on a separate page. He then worked this up at his leisure, gradually building up the density with numerous layers of watercolour, and finally strengthening the whole image with bravura pen and ink work, paying particular attention to the face. At a later date, probably when the idea of a book first occurred to him, he numbered the figures, and wrote a caption in pencil on the backs of many, but not all, of the pages. His tutor, Greiffenhagen, was a portrait painter, and it is obvious that he passed much of his skill on to him. Haswell Miller's style is instantly recognisable, and I think it is the naturalness of the poses and the intense characterisation of the faces, rather than the finer details, although they are there, that make his work stand out among his contemporaries.

The title and sub-title of the book are the ones he originally gave to it; but in spite of the wording of the latter, he continued his sketching right through the war, taking advantage of moments of leave and recuperation from the wound he received in the final advance in 1918, when he was awarded the Military Cross. Most of the plates contain two rows of five or more figures, but from the beginning of the war years he changed this to a single row of larger figures, sometimes with an ornamental border, as though he already had the idea of a book in mind. Early in 1919 he sent a drawing of the peace and wartime uniforms of his regiment to Charles ffoulkes, the secretary of the recently established Imperial War Museum, and as a result was commissioned to paint sixty-five watercolour groups along the same lines. This was probably when one of the then small group of enthusiastic students of uniform,

L. E. Buckell, remarked to a fellow enthusiast: 'Who is this young man who draws soldiers that look like soldiers?' He soon became part of this group, which contained such luminaries as the Reverend Percy Sumner, the historian S. M. Milne, the civil servant and amateur artist P. W. Reynolds, and the professional artists Harry Payne and C. C. P. Lawson. The work of these pioneers came to fruition in 1921 with the founding of the Society for Army Historical Research, which put the study of uniforms on a serious footing. An early member, he was eventually to write the catalogue of the military drawings and paintings in the Royal Collection together with fellow enthusiast Nick Dawnay.

As a child, I spent most of my time drawing and, like Haswell Miller, developed a very keen interest in the same subject, suffering like him from a lack of information; in fact I relied mainly on *The Wonder Book of Soldiers*, cigarette cards supplied by my mother and the occasional Harry Payne postcard. It was not until 1940, when C. C. P. Lawson published the first volume of his *History of the Uniforms of the British Army*, that a serious book on the subject came my way. Through a series of happy coincidences I met 'C. C. P.' while I was still at school; he became a great friend and my *ex officio* professor of military history; and it was through him that I met Haswell Miller, although unfortunately I never got to know him very well.

Haswell Miller's obituary in the *Journal of the Society for Army Historical Research* describes how, well into his nineties, he travelled once a week from his home in Dorset to Whitehall and the offices of the Ogilby Trust, to which, for the last twenty-five years of his life, he was artistic adviser. What is less well known, however – and I have it from an impeccable source – is that on each of these visits he stopped off at Christie's to reminisce with the head porter, Jim Taylor, about military matters in general and to keep an eye on the military lots passing through. The obituary goes on to say that 'he had the most remarkable memory and would immediately recognise a photograph or a painting and identify it'; I do not know whether his sessions with Jim Taylor contributed to this ability or not, but I am sure he enjoyed them.

Working from Colin Sibun's transcription of the author's manuscript notes, I have left Haswell Miller's full page comments very much as he wrote them, but have added my own notes to each army about interesting or unusual features and the introduction of service dress, before and during the First World War. I have also added sections on orders of dress and rank badges. I have virtually rewritten the original captions, simplifying them by reducing them to rank, unit, order of dress and place seen, and filling in the missing identifications. The author himself did not claim total accuracy for the 759 different figures he drew, and in places he noted where he had, or thought he had, made a mistake. It is not surprising therefore that in the process of identification new ones have come to light and, in fairness to him and to the reader, I have included them as and when they occur. Moreover, because of his style, by which the finer details such as headdress badges and rank insignia are difficult to make out, some of the identifications have had to be left vaguer than I would have hoped. Nevertheless, the resulting assemblage of the faces, dress and postures of over seven hundred long-gone soldiers, each recognisably typical of his particular country, is an achievement of which the artist would have been justifiably proud.

I have been greatly helped, in the first place, by Colin Sibun's transcription of Haswell Miller's handwriting, alone a feat of considerable detective work, and in the further checking of the existing captions, and the identification of the missing ones, by my brothers Boris and Andrew, and by Michael Barthorp, Gerardo Girardo Crocini, Jacques de Cartier-d'Yves, Mark van Hattem of the Royal Netherlands Army and Arms Museum, Delft, Pierre Lierneux of the Royal Army Museum, Brussels, Laurent Mirouze, and Alfred Umhey, to all of whom I offer my gratitude.

John Mollo

NOTE: Where possible, except in the captions to the plates, I have put my additions in italics and added (JM) at the end.

INTRODUCTION

There is no system nor any attempt to achieve anything of organisation in this collection and no thought of publication came into my mind until it appeared to arouse interest among a few serious students of the subject, especially perhaps in the general climate of highly coloured 'militaria', where the contemporary document is of little interest.

My critical feeling about the drawings, made from sixty to seventy years ago, is rather odd. In many ways they are very bad and clumsy but I feel that they have in their crudities some qualities that I have lost in such military drawings as I attempt today. Youth cannot be used as an excuse for this shortcoming since the earliest – the Munich figures – were drawn when I was already over twenty-one. Looking back to those student days, I recognise extreme stupidity in refusing to learn by copying the work of the artists whose work I admired – even 'aped': (Edvard Thony, Angelo Jank).

Very oddly, during a stay with one of my professors, a dear friend, at Forte dei Marmi in 1913, it happened that one of the great German artists, Adolf von Hildebrand, became intrigued by some of these drawings and took them away to explore the possibility of publishing them. They were exhibited at Leipzig, the war came, Hildebrand died, my paintings came back perfectly preserved and were more or less forgotten.

A. E. Haswell Miller
London, 1976

UNIFORM IN LIFE

The soldier has disappeared. However, I believe we might be told by authority that we have a larger army than when the soldier, in colourful and meaningful dress, was part of the street scene, or any train load of travellers. Today it is hard to credit that the daily scene of life in cities, towns and even the country had the colourful element of military uniform and that any busy street and every railway platform or music hall would have its proportion of smart soldiers and sailors, proud of the uniform that they were not allowed to wear until they were qualified not to discredit it. This is applicable to all countries. There were essential differences to the scene in various countries. One never saw an officer, who could only be seen in uniform when on parade – when a regiment might be marching through a city or country, particularly recruiting. In France the officer was invisible, as in England, but there were short occasions when they could be seen on the move. Throughout Austria and Hungary it seemed that all officers spent their off duty time in the main promenades of city, town or village – and what elegance. In Germany and Italy the situation was the same except that the national characteristics would find the officer in rather different conditions – perhaps more or less in the café.

The arrival in a 'new' country, especially as a young adventurer in uniform, was a day of great excitement. Where were the Guards? How did one recognise them? Were the cavalry like other countries with hussars and lancers in separate lines or did all the cavalry go into one line following the British scheme?; *Litzen* [*rectangular 'loops' of braid (JM)*] were obviously a mark of Guard units to a certain degree; repeated visits to the uniform shops and show cases; the realisation of the place of the Shako Cockade in the German Army.

On return to England the fresh painted crew that had developed from months in Vienna or Rome; the comparison of notes with mentors like Buckell or Reynolds and the internal opening of a window through one's 'notes'.

This work was not undertaken in any serious spirit. Although its first pages were carried out in Germany, they are a development of childhood's attempts to make a serious collection of drawn and painted military uniforms. In the mid-[eighteen]nineties a boy of my rather nondescript 'class' in Glasgow was not liable to be bored as are the television-sated young of today's generations and my school day recollections are of waiting for the precious hour or two with freedom to read, draw or spend time on an inferior stamp collection. This last persistently lagged behind those of my friends and barely allowed my acceptance as a collector to the lowest rungs of the ladder through my possession of a 'fourpenny [Samoa]'. But few boys drew, and inspired by occasional birthday or Christmas presents of toy soldiers, I drew and recognised subconsciously that there were 'regiments' with strange names and arbitrary uniforms: 'Madras Light Cavalry', 'Bombay Lancers', 'Black Watch'. Added to these were less unattainable treasures in the form of 'scraps' that supplied fascinating details of Life Guards, Grenadier Guards and Black Watch.

Indeed memory brings back pictures of variously shaped boxes of toy soldiers – certainly as far back as the early nineties – which birthdays and Christmas brought. They were distressingly different in scale and I believe I began to draw them in order that this could be adjusted. Very small French Infantry I recall, which aroused questions of my father, resulting in the satisfying knowledge that English wore red coats and blue trousers, and the French blue coats and red trousers. Germans wore all blue and Austrians white or light blue. Russians wore grey or green. (My father, in his youth, had worn a red shirt in Garibaldi's British Volunteers in 1860.) Returning to the toy soldiers, I got on to firmer ground with long boxes of Britain's fine Bengal Lancers and Madras Light Cavalry (whose lances, swords or rifles could move to various positions).

In 1897 I created a complete (exercise) book of the uniforms of the British Army, the 'Army List' being produced by the advertisement of collections of army badges at the back of my 'Lincoln Stamp Album'. I knew nothing of the existence of actual Army Lists. Where I got the vital elementary details from – facings, colours of plumes, busby bags, etc. – I cannot remember. 1897, of course, as Jubilee Year, brought endless pictures of soldiers in the weeklies and I managed to see a tiny proportion of these. I was not pampered and had to fight for information without knowing how to do so – a curious subconscious struggle, in secret, always a little ashamed or feeling it was somehow wrong and wasting valuable time.

GREAT BRITAIN

In 1890 blue serge frocks (patrol jackets) and field service caps (side-caps) were introduced for drill and manoeuvres in mounted regiments; in 1896 a new pattern appeared with shoulder chains but in 1902 blue serge was officially abolished in favour of khaki. It was, however, retained in India (which presumably meant that it was still available for wear on the regiment's return home). By 1914 it was being used as an alternative undress by dismounted units as well.

As a result of the experience gained by the British Army during the Boer War, the wearing of full dress was confined to ceremonial purposes and walking out. In 1902 a khaki service dress was introduced for all occasions not requiring full dress, and was worn with the Brodrick cap (see note to figure 133) or glengarry, until 1905, when the khaki peaked cap was introduced. This became the universal service headdress except in the Scottish regiments. In 1908 the leather bandolier equipment was replaced by a complete set of equipment in khaki webbing, including belt, pouches, haversack, water bottle and backpack, which was worn up to 1937

The use of the khaki service dress was far from universal as had been intended, and, apart from a few men in review order, most of Haswell Miller's British figures are in full dress, used as an undress or walking-out dress, many of them being members of regimental bands, pipes and drums, seen during the Glasgow Exhibition of 1911. There are only twelve British figures shown wearing khaki before the outbreak of war in September 1914. (JM)

ORDERS OF DRESS

Authorities differ on the exact composition of the various orders of dress worn between 1908 and 1914, but the following seven are the ones that appear most frequently in the British plates.

1. Review order. *Full dress with full-dress headdress.*
2. Undress. *Full dress with the forage cap or glengarry and side arms, sometimes with the blue serge frock and sometimes with the khaki service dress tunic introduced in 1902.*
3. Walking-out dress. *As undress but without side arms and usually with a swagger stick or riding whip.*
4. Drill order. *Shell jacket and forage cap or glengarry – red for the Life Guards, blue for the Royal Horse Guards, white for the Foot Guards and Highland regiments. Other*

regiments are shown in this order of dress wearing full dress, with forage cap and white Slade-Wallace belt and pouches.

5. Service dress. *Khaki forage cap or glengarry, khaki jacket or doublet for Scottish regiments, and trousers and puttees, khaki kilt apron and khaki spats for Highland regiments, worn with the 1908 pattern webbing equipment.*
6. Guard order. *Full or service dress with ammunition pouches only. In the Foot Guards, the cloak was worn folded on the back.*
7. Marching order. *Full or service dress with full equipment and backpack. (JM)*

RANK BADGES

As there are no figures of general officers in this section their rank badges are not included.

Field officers
Colonel. *A gold embroidered crown and two stars of the Order of the Bath on each shoulder.*
Lieutenant-Colonel. *A gold embroidered crown and one star of the Order of the Bath on each shoulder.*
Major. *A gold embroidered crown on each shoulder.*

Subaltern officers
Captain. *Three gold embroidered stars of the Order of the Bath on each shoulder.*
Lieutenant. *Two gold embroidered stars of the Order of the Bath on each shoulder.*
Second Lieutenant. *One gold embroidered star of the Order of the Bath on each shoulder.*

With the khaki service dress the rank badges were woven in drab worsted and sewn on the cuff, with four rows of drab worsted braid round the cuff for Colonels, three for Lieutenant-Colonels and Majors, two for Captains, and one for Lieutenants and Second Lieutenants. The badges were set on a three-pointed flap for all except Scottish regiments, who wore them on a 'gauntlet' cuff edged with one to four rows of drab braid.

Warrant officers and NCOs
Staff Sergeant-Major. *A gold embroidered crown on the right arm.*

Acting Sergeant-Major. *A gold embroidered crown above four gold lace inverted chevrons, on the right arm above the cuff.*
Company Sergeant-Major. *A gold embroidered crown above three gold lace chevrons, on the upper right arm.*
Sergeant. *Three gold lace chevrons on the right upper arm.*
Corporal. *Two white worsted braid chevrons, on the right upper arm. On the white drill jacket, the chevrons were red.*
Lance-Corporal. *One white worsted braid chevron, on the right upper arm. On the white drill jacket, the chevron was red.*

Inverted white worsted braid long-service chevrons were worn by all ranks below Sergeant, on the left arm above the cuff, each chevron representing four years' service. On the khaki service dress the rank badges were in the same woven drab braid as used for the NCOs' chevrons. (JM)

Plate 1: figures 1–10

1. Sergeant, Royal Field Artillery, mounted review order. From 1904 men of the Royal Field Artillery wore a coloured girdle as shown here.
2. Trumpeter, Royal Field Artillery, mounted review order.
3. Gunner, Royal Garrison Artillery, review order.
4. Officer, Royal Field Artillery, review order.
5. Officer, Royal Field Artillery, review order.
6. Gunner, Royal Field Artillery, walking-out dress, with trial pattern khaki greatcoat.
7. Gunner, Royal Artillery, service dress.
8. Staff Sergeant, Royal Engineers, walking-out dress with blue 'serge frock' (patrol jacket).
9. Gunner, Royal Field Artillery, back view of figure 6.
10. Gunner, Royal Horse Artillery, walking-out dress.

This page must have been drawn in early summer, 1910. I remember returning home on a Saturday afternoon after having seen, and followed for some distance, a Field Battery or Brigade of the Royal Artillery that was carrying out a recruiting march in full dress. It was, I believe, an unusual thing for such a unit to form part of the garrison at Maryhill, and I think it was there for a very short period. In any case I had, I think, never seen a regular field artillery brigade on parade.

I had returned from a year's study in Munich in September 1909. There I had made the earliest pages of this record, and it was on this Saturday that it occurred to me that the principle of recording such uniforms as I encountered, no matter what order of dress it might be, should be carried on at home.

Actually, figures 1, 2, 4 and 5 were the only ones inspired by the recruiting march. In the evening I thought I might find some more material to complete the page and went for a walk in the town, finding the interesting new trial khaki greatcoat worn by a soldier. This was the only time I have ever seen this garment and I guessed it to have been something designed for mounted troops. I never saw this greatcoat again and suppose that economy prevailed over the handsome elaborations of the cape, the buttoned pockets, double cuffs and full back. I think figure 7 may have been on barrack guard but as regards the other figures I do not recall the occasions on which they were seen. The girdle shown in figures 1 and 2 was a comparatively new feature of Royal Artillery uniform. It may be that I should have added the white sword slings appearing from under the jacket as in figure 10.

Khaki was relatively strange, seen less than coloured uniforms. It was not liable to be worn except as actual service dress, not even on the barrack square where drill and other training would be carried out in whitish or brown canvas.

It may be noticed that in all cavalry figures or mounted ranks there is an insistence on the appearance of the sword slings. This was I think essential in 'walking-out' dress as proof that the wearer had the honour of carrying arms. Today (1975) this aspect of uniform is forgotten. We have the strange appearance of the King's Troop RHA mounting guard in Whitehall without sword slings. The consequence being (if one exercises the imagination) a short period during which the sword, either unsheathed or returned to the scabbard, has to be tucked under the soldier's arm or carried somehow awkwardly.

Plate 2: figures 11–20

These figures must have been drawn in Glasgow in 1910 or 1911 for I seem to remember the odd one from the Glasgow National Exhibition of the latter year.

11. Drummer, Royal Dublin Fusiliers, undress.
12. Back view of figure 11.
13. Trooper, 11th Hussars, walking-out dress.
14. Trooper, 11th Hussars, walking-out dress with patrol jacket.
15. Trooper, 3rd Dragoon Guards, walking-out dress.
16. Corporal, 16th Lancers, walking-out dress with patrol jacket.
17. Piper, Argyll and Sutherland Highlanders, drill order with white jacket.

18. Staff Sergeant, Highland Light Infantry, service dress.
19. Trooper, 2nd Dragoons (Royal Scots Greys), walking-out dress.
20. Trooper, 7th Hussars, walking-out dress.

The first two figures show the front and back of a bugler or drummer of the Royal Dublin Fusiliers, very normal and without the elaborations of braid sported by some regiments. The drummer's lace has red crowns woven into the white. He also has the narrower lace of red and white on the pointed cuff and (not visible) at the base of the collar.

It must be kept in mind that between band, drums and soldiers, especially 'boys', there was a certain coming and going with the former, naturally, being on trial. It was not impossible to find a well-dressed drummer or bugler in the regimental band alongside a soldier without the piped bandsman's tunic or doublet. Until it appeared that a bugler was going to be a stayer there was a natural hesitation to go to the expense of the elaboration of his dress.

This was my first observation of the introduction of the purely decorative buglers'/drummers' dress cords, which initially followed the regulation red-yellow-blue for 'royal' regiments and plain green for 'non-royal' regiments, but which were soon to be seen in fanciful regimental colours.

Figures 13 and 14 show the same man, evidently showing off two different orders of dress. The 11th Prince Albert's Own Hussars is the only Hussar regiment to wear crimson overalls and little comment is required on these figures. I should not have been surprised to see the fall of the cap lines loop from the neck plaited, but apparently the wearer I saw did not adopt this quirk. The other end of the lines, in full dress attached to the busby, under the bag, is here fastened to the bottom button of the jacket. About this time Hussar and Lancer regiments seem to have adopted regimental methods of looping the headdress ends to certain buttons, or elsewhere on the tunic; this can be seen on figures 16 and 20. I would also have expected to find figure 14 wearing his cap lines to brighten up his serge. I don't know to what extent the wearing of the serge for 'walking out' may have been frowned on. Figure 14 tells us that the 11th Hussars wore chain epaulettes on their serges while figure 16 shows yellow cords. The latter wears his lines rather oddly and what happened behind can only be guessed. From an almost indecipherable note beside him I gather that I had seen him in his full dress tunic, red of course in the 16th. I can hardly think that lines would have been worn this way with the Lancer tunic.

Figure 17 outraged me when I encountered him in the National Exhibition (1911). Only recently, some sixty years mellowed, I have decided he was one of those enterprising soldiers who had his own ideas on uniform. He ought to be a piper of the Argylls but chose to wear the diced glengarry and the red and white hose denied to all pipers since the middle of the nineteenth century for some odd reason, and only now creeping back. The band sporran has been improved on, and I cannot reconcile it with any pattern known to me. Experience has shown me (since 1911) that there has always been a tendency for the Scottish soldier to borrow plaids and pipers' belts in order to be photographed.

Figure 18 is a Staff Sergeant of the Highland Light Infantry in the regulation khaki jacket with twisted braid shoulder cords and gauntlet form laced cuffs.

Figures 19 and 20 require little comment. They are wearing correct walking-out uniforms for the Royal Scots Greys and 7th Queen's Own Hussars. At that time a cavalry soldier (or any sword carrier) would never be seen without sword slings.

Plate 3: figures 21–31

21. Bandsman, 2nd Bn, Argyll and Sutherland Highlanders, drill order.
22. Private, 7th Bn, Black Watch (TF), walking-out dress.
23. Officer, Northumberland Hussars, undress with frock coat.
24. Piper, 2nd Bn, Argyll and Sutherland Highlanders, review order.
25. Piper, Scottish Horse (Imperial Yeomanry), review order. May 1911.
26. Trooper, Queen's Own Royal Glasgow Yeomanry, review order. May 1911. Whole regiment is not supplied with this dress.
27. Private, King's Own Scottish Borderers, walking-out dress.
28. Bandsman, Gordon Highlanders, undress.
29. Staff Sergeant, Northumberland Hussars, walking-out dress with 'pill-box' cap, which officially went out in 1902 when khaki came in.
30. Sergeant Piper, 2nd Bn, Argyll and Sutherland Highlanders, review order.
31. Private, 2nd Bn, Argyll and Sutherland Highlanders, drill order (service dress doublet with the 1908 pattern web belt and bayonet frog, worn with trews).

Plate 4: figures 31a–40

31a. Band Sergeant, Royal Irish Fusiliers, undress, wearing the Queen's and King's South Africa War Medals. Glasgow, July 1911.
32. Bandsman, Royal Irish Fusiliers, undress. London, 1913.
33. Bandmaster, Royal Irish Fusiliers, officers' undress with frock coat.
34. Band Drummer, Royal Irish Fusiliers, review order.
35. Corporal, Strathcona's Horse (Canada), walking-out dress with scarlet serge frock. Glasgow, July 1911.
36. Sergeant, Queen's Own Royal Glasgow Yeomanry, drill order.
37. Private, Royal Canadian Regiment, walking-out dress. Glasgow, June 1911.
38. Captain of an unknown regiment, possibly Canadian, undress with greatcoat. Seen in Glasgow.
39. Sergeant, New Zealand Mounted Rifles, walking-out dress.
40. Bandmaster, 5th Bn, Highland Light Infantry (TF), undress.

Plate 5: figures 41–50

41. Sergeant-Major, Kaffarian Rifles (South Africa), walking-out dress, with the 'Best shot in company' proficiency badge on his left lower arm. His medals include the Distinguished Conduct Medal (DCM) and the two medals (Queen's and King's) for the South African War 1899–1902.
42. Bandmaster, 2nd Bn, Highland Light Infantry, undress.
43. Band Lance-Corporal, 2nd Bn, Highland Light Infantry, drill order with white jacket.
44. Pipe-Major, 2nd Bn, Highland Light Infantry, review order.
45. Bandmaster, 2nd Bn, Highland Light Infantry, drill order, with red jacket.
46. Bandmaster, 2nd Bn, Highland Light Infantry, front view of figure 42. The Bandmaster wears the four inverted chevrons of an Acting Segeant-Major with a special badge instead of a crown.
47. Drummer, 2nd Bn, Highland Light Infantry, review order.
48. Bandsman, 2nd Bn, Cameronians (Scottish Rifles), undress.
49. Band Sergeant, 2nd Bn, Highland Light Infantry, drill order.
50. Private, Kimberley Regiment (South Africa), walking-out dress. His medal may be the 1902 Coronation Medal.

Plate 6: figures 51–60

51. Bandsman, Gordon Highlanders, undress.
52. Piper, 2nd Bn, Highland Light Infantry, drill order.
53. Bandmaster, Gordon Highlanders, undress.
54. Sergeant, Argyll and Sutherland Highlanders, drill order with white jacket.
55. Trooper, Cape Mounted Rifles (South Africa), walking-out dress in khaki service dress and field service cap.
56. Corporal, Seaforth Highlanders, drill order.
57. Bandsman, Royal Marine Light Infantry, Portsmouth Division, undress. The Portsmouth Division wore small silver Prince of Wales feathers over the cap badge as shown here. The medal he is wearing appears to be the Distinguished Conduct Medal (DCM).
58. Piper, Gordon Highlanders, review order.
59. Lieutenant, 5th Bn, Cameronians (TF), formerly the 1st Lanarkshire Rifle Volunteers, review order.
60. Signal Sergeant, 4th Bn, Royal Scots (TF), Queen's Edinburgh Rifles, undress.

Plate 7: figures 61–70

61. Sergeant, Irish Guards, walking-out dress with greatcoat.
62. Band Corporal of Horse, 1st Life Guards, undress. His rank is indicated by the gold aiguillette on his left shoulder.
63. Bandmaster, 1st Life Guards, undress with frock coat. The fringe at the waist between the buttons is also to be found on the tunics and pelisses of Austrian Hussars.
64. Bandmaster, Royal Artillery, undress with frock coat.
65. Band Drummer, Scots Guards, undress.
66. Bandmaster, Seaforth Highlanders, drill order with white jacket.
67. Band Sergeant, 8th Bn, Durham Light Infantry (TF), undress.
68. Officer, Coldstream Guards, undress with greatcoat.
69. Band Sergeant, Coldstream Guards, undress.
70. Sergeant, Imperial Light Horse (South Africa), undress with patrol jacket and 'Best shot in company' badge on left lower arm.

Plate 8: figures 71–82

71. Boy Bandsman, Queen Victoria Memorial School, Dunblane, full dress and glengarry.
72. Bandsman, Royal Engineers (Chatham), undress. Blue velvet facings; shoulder cords; back similar to

Guards pattern of bearskin in full dress; braid goes right round cuff, unlike 73.

73. Bandsman, Royal Field Artillery (Woolwich), undress. Blue shoulder straps with gold braid edging.
74. Bandmaster, Royal Scots Fusiliers, undress.
75. Bandmaster, Royal Engineers, undress with frock coat.
76. Band Corporal, Royal Scots Fusiliers, review order, with two long-service chevrons on the lower left arm.
77. Staff Sergeant Instructor, Army Gymnastic Staff, walking-out dress. His medals include the two South Africa War medals and the Africa General Service Medal 1902.
78. Pipe Major, Queen Victoria School, Dunblane, review order.
79. Boy Piper, Queen Victoria School, Dunblane, full dress with glengarry.
80. Boy Drummer, Queen Victoria School, Dunblane, full dress with glengarry.
81. Band Sergeant, Queen Victoria School, Dunblane, undress.
82. Boy Drum Major, Queen Victoria School, Dunblane, review order.

Plate 9: figures 83–92

83. Corporal, 9th Bn, Royal Scots (TF), drill order.
84. Sergeant-Major, Irish Guards, undress.
85. Lieutenant, Queen's Own Royal Glasgow Yeomanry, review order.
86. Band Sergeant, 2nd Bn, Royal Northumberland Fusiliers, review order.
87. Band Sergeant, 2nd Bn, Royal Northumberland Fusiliers, undress with two South Africa War medals.
88. Band Drummer, 2nd Bn, Royal Northumberland Fusiliers, undress.
89. Private, 1/1st, Highland Cyclist Battalion (TF), service dress with brown leather equipment. Note the holster holding what is probably a bicycle tool kit, the non-regulation stockings with red garter tabs, and the spats.
90. Sergeant, 1/1st, Highland Cyclist Battalion (TF), walking-out dress.
91. Band Sergeant, Royal Scots Fusiliers, undress.
92. Piper, Royal Scots, drill order with white jacket.

Plate 10: figures 93–103

93. Major, 2nd Bn, Argyll and Sutherland Highlanders, dismounted review order.
94. Lieutenant, 2nd Bn, Argyll and Sutherland Highlanders, review order.
95. Bandsman, 2nd Bn, Argyll and Sutherland Highlanders, review order.
96. Drum Major, 2nd Bn, Argyll and Sutherland Highlanders, review order.
97. Drummer, 2nd Bn, Argyll and Sutherland Highlanders, review order.
98. Band Sergeant, Royal Marine Light Infantry, Portsmouth Division, undress with patrol jacket.
99. Private, 8th Bn, Highland Light Infantry (TF), walking-out dress.
100. Pipe Major, 2nd Bn, Argyll and Sutherland Highlanders, review order.
101. Bandsman (or Trooper), 1st Life Guards, walking-out dress cloaked.
102. Trooper, 1st Life Guards, walking-out dress.
103. Private, 3rd (Territorial) Scottish General Hospital, Royal Army Medical Corps, service dress.

This is an instructive plate. All the figures were seen in early summer 1911. The 2nd Argyll and Sutherland Highlanders (93rd) had just come home from India and were resplendent examples of the old army. I think that the parade at which the 93rd figures appeared was the occasion of the opening of the Glasgow Exhibition. The six figures shown introduce aspects of the regimental Highland uniform in exaggerated form, and warn the student what must be looked for in the various ranks and appointments within the various battalions of the eleven Scottish regiments. Of the five kilted figures, four will be found to be wearing sporrans of different patterns. That worn by figure 94 is the normal officers' pattern worn in all orders of dress except levée, mess and evening (or any occasion where gaiters were not worn). A similar one was worn by Sergeants and Warrant Officers in all kilted orders of dress. Figure 95 is a bandsman and has a special sporran – whether the Band Sergeant wore this I do not know, nor did I note the Bandmaster's dress, which was probably the same as that of an officer but with the red hackle. This last detail of dress when worn by bands may be of a different colour. The body plaid was normal wear for all bands, pipers and drum majors but not drummers (who wore bonnet and sporran of the rank and file type as shown in figure 97).

I have shown the plaid falling to front and rear in these figures; this may be correct since I have drawn the Pipe Major with his plaid folded back to avoid difficulties with the pipes. The Drum Major had a white hackle and a normally laced doublet, which proved to be the sergeant's or private's one converted by the detail of the cuff lace following the short white piped slit at the back of the gauntlet. The three-tailed silver-topped sporran was worn only by the Drum Major and Pipe Major of the 2nd Battalion, those of the same ranks in the 1st Battalion being of a normal pattern. The kilt of the Drum Major shows the emerald green side panel with bows and rosettes as worn on all kilts for the rank of sergeant and upwards. This will be seen on figures 94 and 100.

The Drummer (figure 97) has a normal drummer's or bugler's doublet with broad crown lace and narrow red and white lace at the base of the collar and button hole loops, on cuffs and pocket flaps. An interesting feature is that the Argyll and Sutherland Highlanders' drummers faithfully wore the sporran (same pattern as the rank and file) slinging it round the rear of the drum; other regiments were apt to discard the sporran. The Pipe Major (figure 100) has special battalion pattern wings on his doublet. Pipers' and Pipe Majors' wings can be expected to be almost invariably of battalion pattern before 1914, even those of Territorial battalions. I have been very careless about the hose and gaiters. The top diamond on the turnover should invariably be red and the point of the gaiter ends should fall from the lower point of that diamond. As regards figure 93, I see that I had noted 'Field Officer, Dismounted Parade'. This may account for his wearing a shoulder sword belt and a dirk in his waist belt. It should be noted that this regiment wears the sword belt over the sash, unlike all other Scottish regiments at the time. Also the Pipe Major adhered rigidly to wearing his sash on the 'non-commissioned' right shoulder.

Figure 98 was presumably the Band Sergeant-Major of the Portsmouth Division of the Royal Marine Light Infantry. Probably they were playing at the Glasgow Exhibition and he would be seeing that all was properly organised before a performance. The rank badge is odd; on his red tunic I think he only had ordinary chevrons. Figure 99 is a Private of the 8th (Lanark) Territorial Battalion, Highland Light Infantry, the only battalion of the regiment to wear the diced glengarry. It was apparently issued with the 1904 leather equipment. Otherwise the battalion wore normal HLI uniform. In figure 101 (1st or 2nd Life Guards) the red cloak is ill drawn, and not understood; probably he should have white gloves. Figure 102, also 1st or 2nd Life Guards, is not a characteristic figure; at that date no cap badge was worn.

Figure 103 is of the Royal Army Medical Corps (Territorial), 3rd Scottish General Hospital. It must be remembered that in 1911 khaki was not seen very much, and the equipment does not seem to have been worked out since he wears a full-dress pouch belt and sword, old white canvas haversack and a 1904 water bottle.

Plate 11: figures 104–115

104. Drum-Major, 9th Bn, Highland Light Infantry (TF), review order. May 1914.
105. Bandmaster, 9th Bn, Highland Light Infantry (TF), review order. May 1914.
106. Band Staff Sergeant, 9th Bn, Highland Light Infantry (TF), review order. May 1914.
107. Field Officer, 9th Bn, Highland Light Infantry (TF), review order. May 1914.
108. Field Officer, Highland Light Infantry, review order.
109. Private, Grenadier Guards, guard order.
110. Major, Cameronians, service dress with the triple line of khaki braid edging the cuff and the crown showing his rank. April 1914.
111. Lieutenant, 5th Bn, Argyll and Sutherland Highlanders (TF), service dress. 1910.
112. Lieutenant, Grenadier Guards, guard order cloaked. 1910.
113. Band Corporal, 5th Bn, Cameronians (TF), undress. May 1914.
114. Captain, 9th Bn, Highland Light Infantry (TF), undress with patrol jacket. May 1914.
115. Private, York and Lancaster Regiment, with eight years' service, walking-out dress. 1913–14.

Plate 12: figures 115a–123

115a. Pipe Major, 5th Bn, Cameronians (TF), review order.
115b. Bandsman, Royal Marines, undress, with white cover to forage cap. The RMLI and the RMA were amalgamated in 1923 to form the Royal Marines.
116. Lance-Corporal, East Yorkshire Regiment, walking-out dress with three service chevrons on the left lower arm. He wears the two South Africa War medals and the Africa Service Medal.
117. Bandsman, 10th Bn, King's Liverpool Regiment, the Liverpool Scottish (TF), review order.
118. Drummer, 5th Bn, Cameronians (TF), review order.
119. Sergeant, Royal Scots, review order. In 1902 the two Lowland Scottish Regiments, the Royal Scots and the King's Own Scottish Borderers, changed their former helmets for the blue wide-topped 'Kilmarnock' bonnet.
120. Piper, 1st Bn, Cameronians, review order.
121. Bugler, 1st Bn, Cameronians, review order.
122. Drummer, 8th Bn, Cameronians (TF), full dress.
123. Bandmaster, 2nd Bn, Cameronians, undress with dark green patrol jacket.

Plate 13: figures 124–133b

124. Sergeant, 1st Royal Dragoons, undress, seen on recruiting duties in London in 1912. The cap band is cloth, not velvet as for Dragoon Guards.
125. Trooper, 2nd Life Guards, drill order.
126. Sergeant, Irish Guards, undress with red serge frock. His tunic is clearly not the full-dress one. It has no white piping to the collar, no shoulder straps, only a red cord on the right to retain his sash, and no cuff slash. He wears the two South Africa War medals and what looks like the Distinguished Conduct Medal.
127. Drummer, Welsh Regiment, review order.
128. Bugler, Welsh Regiment, undress.
129. Band Sergeant, Queen's Royal West Surrey Regiment, review order.
130. A member of the Army Recruiting Staff, walking-out dress.
131. NCO, Military Foot Police, walking-out dress.
132. Trooper, 1st Life Guards, drill order with two long-service chevrons.
133. Gunner, Royal Marine Artillery, walking-out dress with Brodrick cap.
133a. Bandsman, 20th Hussars, undress.
133b. Gunner, Royal Marine Artillery, drill order with Brodrick cap in white cover.

The Brodrick cap, seen in figure 133, was introduced in 1902. It was a broad-topped, peakless cap, supposed to have been inspired by the peakless forage caps of the German Army. Blue, except for some cavalry regiments, it had a curved patch in front in the regimental facing colour on which the cap badge was placed, behind a blue flap, piped in the regimental colour for privates, and in gold for NCOs. Although comfortable to wear, it never really caught on and was superseded by the khaki peaked cap in 1905. For some reason the Royal Marines retained theirs and a newspaper photograph of October 1914 shows them returning from Ostend wearing them with blue patrol jackets and khaki webbing equipment. (JM)

Plate 14: figures 134–143

134. Corporal, Royal Horse Guards, drill order.
135. Sergeant, 5th Dragoon Guards, walking-out dress with 'Marksman, Best Shooting Squadron in the Regiment' badge on lower right arm. He is wearing the two South Africa War medals.
136. Staff Sergeant, Irish Guards, undress with patrol jacket.
137. Officer, Queen's Royal West Surrey Regiment, review order, two South Africa War medals.
138. Officer, 20th Hussars, undress with frock coat.
139. Gunner, Royal Marine Artillery, walking-out dress with Brodrick cap.
140. Private, Welsh Regiment, review order.
140a. Private, Dorsetshire Regiment, walking-out dress.
141. Lance Sergeant, Irish Guards, drill order with white jacket. In this order of dress his white chevrons are edged in red.
142. Bugler, King's Shropshire Light Infantry, undress. The tunic collar and cuffs should be dark blue.
143. Trooper, 12th Lancers, walking-out dress.

Plate 15: figures 144–154

144. Pipe-Major, 1st Bn, Cameronians, review order.
145. Bugler, 1st Bn, Cameronians, review order.
146. Private, Cameron Highlanders, walking-out dress with two South Africa War medals.
147. Trooper, 6th Dragoon Guards, walking-out dress.
148. Drummer, Coldstream Guards, guard order.
149. Private, 5th Bn, Cameronians (TF), khaki service dress with glengarry and 1908 webbing equipment.
150. Drummer, Queen's Royal West Surrey Regiment, review order.
151. Officer, Welsh Regiment, review order.
152. Officer, 1st Bn, Cameronians, undress.
153. Officer, 5th Bn, Cameronians (TF).
154. Field Officer, 1st Bn, Cameronians, mounted review order.

Plate 16: figures 155–166

155. Bandsman, Royal Inniskilling Fusiliers, undress. November 1913.
156. Bandmaster, Royal Inniskilling Fusiliers, undress with frock coat. November 1913.
157. Band Sergeant, Royal Inniskilling Fusiliers, review order. November 1913.
158. Bugle Major, 5th Bn, Cameronians (TF), undress. 1912.
159. Private, Reserve Battalion, Royal Fusiliers, walking-out dress. August 1912.
160. Private, Rifle Brigade, marksman with twelve years' service, undress. August 1912. He is wearing four medals including the two South Africa War medals.
161. Captain, Scots Guards, review order. August 1913.
162. Major, 5th Bn, Cameronians (TF), mounted review order.
163. Captain, Scottish Horse (Yeomanry), undress with Kilmarnock bonnet and greatcoat. April 1912.

164. Staff Captain, undress with patrol jacket. July 1912.
165. Bandsman, Scots Guards, walking-out dress. 1911.
166. Acting Sergeant-Major, Cameronians (permanent staff of a Territorial battalion), khaki service dress with greatcoat and glengarry. December 1913.

Plate 17: figures 167–179

This drawing, along with five others, in the one frame, was exhibited at Leipzig in 1914, and, caught by the war, was 'interned' for the duration. It was returned intact in 1919, and the frame remained untouched until 1953, when it fell ... and being broken the drawings were returned to the collection.

167. Pipe Major, Royal Scots Fusiliers, review order. Glasgow, December 1913.
168. Sergeant, 1st Bn, Middlesex Regiment, walking-out dress. London, August 1913.
169. Quartermaster Sergeant, Cameronians, review order with the Queen's South Africa War Medal. Glasgow, January 1914.
170. Major, 5th Bn, Highland Light Infantry (TF), undress with patrol jacket and glengarry. Glasgow, 1910.
171. Captain, Army Service Corps, mess kit with short khaki greatcoat. Glasgow, December 1913. This seems to be a shorter version of the 'British Warm', which originated in India under the title 'Coats, Troops, British, Warm'. He is wearing his rank badges on the shoulder strap.
172. Bandmaster, 1st Bn, Cameronians, review order. Glasgow, February 1914.
173. Boy Piper, Black Watch, undress, service dress with glengarry and trews. Edinburgh, 1911.
174. Piper, 1st Bn, Cameronians, review order. Glasgow, February 1914.
175. Private, King's Royal Rifle Corps, walking-out dress, with three long-service chevrons. He is wearing the two South Africa War medals. London, August 1913.
176. Second Lieutenant, Royal Scots Fusiliers, review order. Glasgow, July 1914.
177. Pipe Band Drummer, Highland Light Infantry, drill order with white jacket. Glasgow, July 1911.
178. Sergeant-Major, 1st Bn, Cameronians, review order with the Queen's South Africa War Medal. Glasgow, February 1914.
179. Private, 1st Bn, Gloucestershire Regiment, walking-out dress. London, January 1914. Note the 'back badge' worn on the cap by this regiment in memory of their back-to-back stand against French cavalry at the Battle of Alexandria in 1801.

Plate 18: figures 180–191

180. Trooper, Lanarkshire Yeomanry, walking-out dress. June 1914.
181. Trooper, Scottish Horse, dismounted review order. June 1914.
182. Front view of preceding figure showing the two South Africa War medals being worn.
183. Bandsman, Cameron Highlanders, undress.
184. Pipe Major, Scots Guards, review order.
185. Private, Royal Army Medical Corps, undress.
186. Trooper, Ayrshire Yeomanry, undress. June 1914.
187. Piper, 7th Bn, Cameronians (TF), review order. June 1914.
188. Private, 2nd Bn, Seaforth Highlanders, review order. June 1914.
189. Sergeant, Seaforth Highlanders, drill order with white jacket.
190. Bandsman, Royal Artillery, undress.
191. Private, Duke of Wellington's Regiment, undress.

Plate 19: figures 192–204

192. Acting Sergeant-Major, Army Service Corps, walking-out dress. March 1914. From 1904 the Army Service Corps wore a girdle in blue with yellow and white stripes.
193. Sergeant, Scots Guards, undress. March 1914.
194. Staff Sergeant (Gymnastics Instructor), 5th Bn, Cameronians (TF), review order. March 1914.
195. Sergeant-Major, Glasgow University Officer Training Corps, undress with khaki service dress doublet and khaki spats. April 1912.
196. Trooper, 17th Lancers, dismounted review order. May 1914.
197. NCO, Army Veterinary Corps, mounted undress with patrol jacket.
198. Trooper, Lothians and Border Horse, walking-out dress. August 1914.
199. Private, Glasgow University Officer Training Corps, khaki marching order.
200. Officer, Highland Light Infantry, undress with glengarry, khaki shirt and tie, khaki service dress jacket, and tartan trews.
201. Cadet, Kelvinside Academy Officer Training Corps, full dress with glengarry. April 1914.
202. Cadet Sergeant, Glasgow Academy Officer Training Corps, drill order with khaki service dress tunic and glengarry. May 1914.
203. Trooper, 1st Life Guards, review order. May 1914.

204. Trooper, Lothians and Border Horse, review order. August 1914.

Plate 20: figures 205–215

Although all except figure 215 are unfinished, and without captions, this plate is included as it gives a very good idea of how Haswell Miller worked. Figures 211–214 are preliminary sketches in pencil. The artist notes that they were the 'Half-hearted continuation of something started in 1914'. Figures 205–210 show the next stage, the gradual addition of colour and the working up of the faces. The completed figure 215, dated 1918, is particularly interesting as it depicts an officer of the Highland Light Infantry (as was Haswell Miller himself), attached to the Dorsetshire Regiment, at the end of the war, very smartly turned out with all the appropriate battle insignia. This is very much what Haswell Miller himself must have looked like and may possibly have been intended as a self-portrait. (JM)

205. Trumpeter, Royal Engineers, undress with forage cap.
206. Piper, Scots Guards, full dress with glengarry.
207. Officer of a Highland regiment, full dress with what looks like a glengarry.
208. General Officer, undress with frock coat.
209. Infantry Officer, undress with frock coat.
210. Infantry Officer, review order.
211. Trumpeter, Scots Greys, review order.
212. Back view of the same.
213. Officer, Royal Army Medical Corps, review order. Compare this figure with figure 1 on plate 21.
214. Field Officer of a Scottish regiment, mounted full dress.
215. Field Officer, Highland Light Infantry, service dress with Kilmarnock and tartan breeches. By the end of the war the custom had crept in of wearing officers' rank badges on the shoulder straps instead of the cuffs, as had been the custom in the Foot Guards ever since the introduction of khaki.

Plate 21

The full-dress figures were sketched in roughly in 1914. The four Canadians were roughed in at the end of the war from notes made at home and in France. The Canadians were very confused – as I was – and I think it may be that nobody is at all clear. Individuals bought what they thought correct.

There is a definite change of style from plate 20 in this and the following three plates. Instead of the two rows of five small figures, we now have a single row of larger, much more finished figures, set within a border with the title written below. This new wartime and post-war format can be seen in several of the foreign plates, which seems to suggest that the artist already had some idea of publication in mind. (JM)

Figures, from left to right:
1. Officer, Royal Army Medical Corps, review order. 1914.
2–5. Four figures of Canadian Scottish Regiments in variations of service dress.
6. Officer, 2nd Dragoons (Scots Greys), review order. 1914.
7. Officer, Lancashire Fusiliers, review order with two South Africa War medals. 1914.

Plate 22

This drawing was made while I was for several months at a school of instruction for NCOs and others, run by the Irish Guards, the instructors being from the 65th Division and the Drill Sergeants from the Irish Guards.

Figures, from left to right:
1. Officer, 15th (Service) Bn, Royal Welsh Fusiliers (1st London Welsh), service dress. London, 1917. This officer wears the traditional Royal Welsh Fusiliers' black flash on the back of his tunic, and blue and red cloth shoulder titles above a yellow battle insignia patch.
2. Lieutenant, 48th Highlanders (Canada), service dress with battle insignia for 3rd Brigade, 1st Canadian Division. London, February 1917.
3. Lieutenant, Australian Light Horse, mounted service dress. London, February 1917.
4. Piper, Irish Guards, walking-out dress with khaki Kilmarnock service dress doublet and 1908 pattern webbing belt. Brentwood, February 1917.
5. Trooper, 19th Alberta Horse (Canada), mounted service dress with brass letters 'AH' on a yellow shoulder strap. Glasgow, October 1914.

Plate 23: Canada, Australia and New Zealand

Figures, from left to right:
1. Trooper, New Zealand Infantry, service dress. Brentwood, February 1917.
2. Private, 72nd Highlanders (Canada), service dress with glengarry. Glasgow, October 1914.

3. Private, 5th Royal Scots (Canada), walking-out dress with two South Africa War medals.
4. Private, Australian Forces, service dress. London, February 1917.
5. Trooper, Canterbury (?) Mounted Rifles (New Zealand), khaki drill foreign service dress and Wolseley helmet with unit patch on the side. London, 1915.

Plate 24: India, South Africa and Canada

Figures, from left to right:
1. Captain, Indian Lancers, service dress with khaki kurta and forage cap.
2. Major, Scottish Company, Prince Alfred's Guards (South Africa), mounted service dress. London, 1917.
3. Gunner, Canadian Field Artillery, service dress with bandolier equipment. London, 1916. The green cap band and shoulder straps were worn when the first Canadians appeared in France.
4. Officer, 58th Vaughan's Rifles (Frontier Force), Indian Army, khaki service dress with black Sam Browne with double braces and rifle-green puttees.
5. Private, Scottish Battalion (South Africa), khaki walking-out dress. London, 1916.
6. Private, 8th Canadian Infantry Battalion, khaki service dress, British-made jacket with C on collar, and the soft version of the khaki forage cap. Battle insignia for the 2nd Brigade, 1st Canadian Division. Brentwood, 1917.

Plate 25: 7th (Blythswood) Battalion, Highland Light Infantry (TF), 157 Brigade, 52nd (Lowland) Division (TF)

This can hardly be held to belong to the general character of the series, but the message is similar. I made this drawing while attached to the 4th (Special Reserve) Battalion of the HLI at Forfar, in January 1919, more or less recovered from wounds that brought me back from the final, and to us incredible, advance in France. I happened to read of the projected Imperial War Museum, and seeing demobilisation ahead I thought of trying to sell the idea of a record of dress and equipment to the proposed museum and sent this to Charles Foulkes. Oddly enough it came off and resulted in my being commissioned to make some eighty groups (at six guineas a time). After some fifty years a little more interest seems to have arisen in them and some are reproduced as postcards; most of the time they seem to have decorated the precincts of the 'Gentlemen', etc. My first idea – as here – was the very optimistic one of making a group for every unit with a uniform of its own, showing its pre-war uniform as well.

Figures, from left to right:
1. Sergeant, church parade order. 1914.
2. Lieutenant (Orderly Officer), undress with glengarry and special regimental pattern patrol jacket. 1914.
3. Corporal, order of dress for patrols in France; marks as worn June to September 1918; sacking round bayonet; cap comforters also worn; equipment seldom.
4. Lieutenant, France; marks as amended October 1918; badges worn, sometimes polished; brown boots or puttees; rank on cuffs or shoulder straps.
5. Private, as for Gallipoli 1915 and Palestine 1916–17; foreign service dress with Wolseley helmet with patch of regimental tartan on the left side only. Khaki serge service dress was issued in winter; steel helmet and short-barrelled rifles were issued in November 1917.

Plate 1

Plate 2

Plate 3

Plate 4

Plate 5

Plate 6

Plate 7

Plate 8

Plate 9

Plate 10

Plate 11

Plate 12

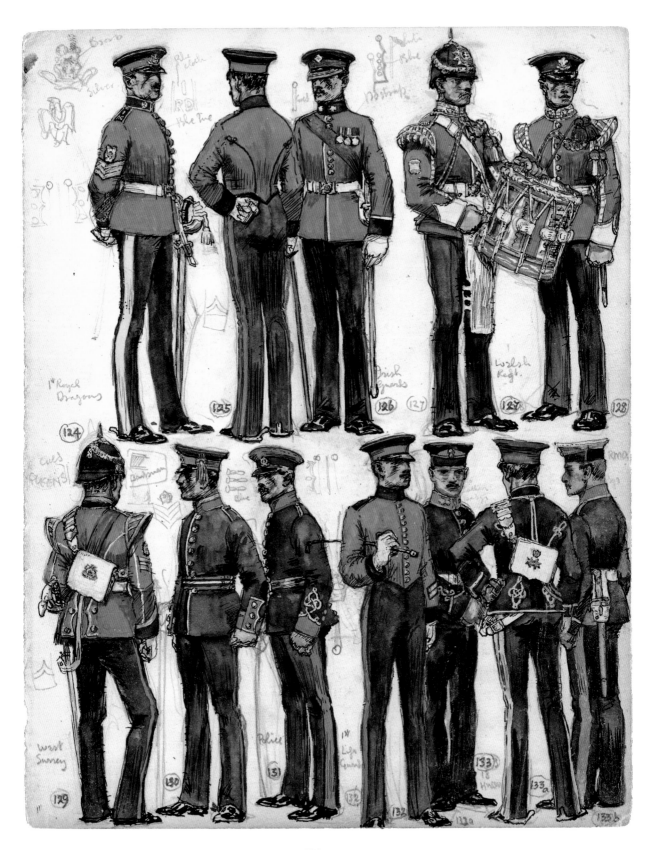

Plate 13

Plate 14

Plate 15

Plate 16

Plate 17

Plate 18

Plate 19

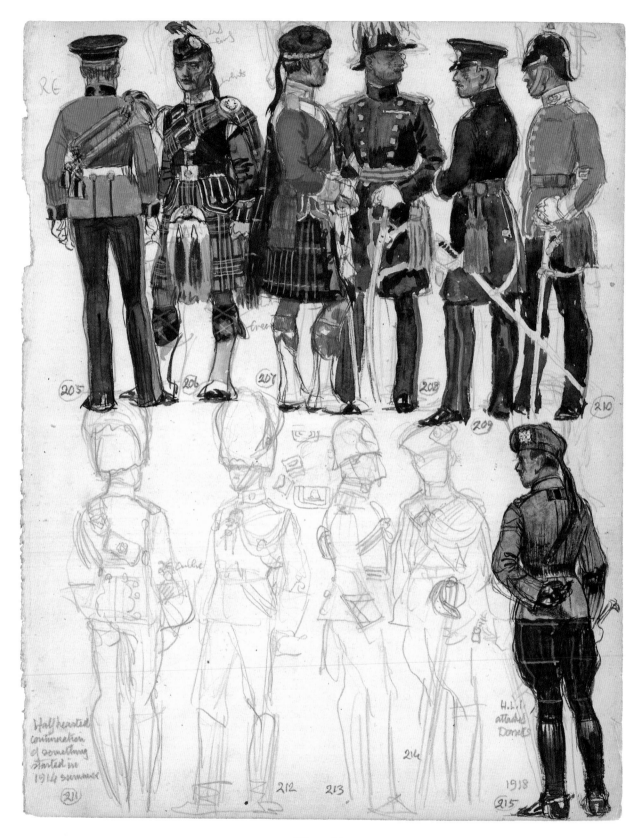

RG

205   206   207   208   209   210

Half hearted
continuation
of something
started in
1914 summer
211   212   213   214

H.L.I.
attached
Dorsets

1918
215

Plate 20

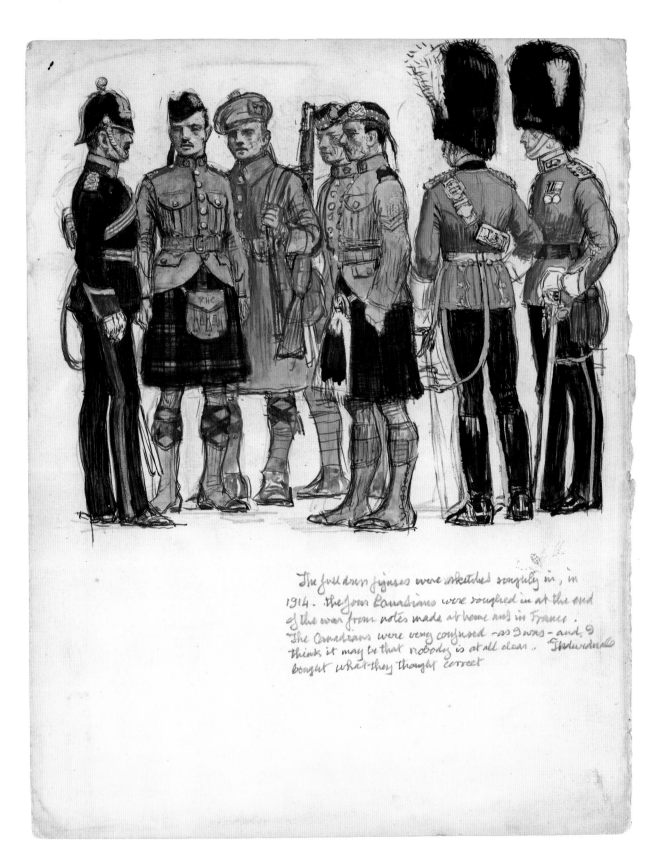

The full dress figures were sketched roughly in, in
1914. The four Canadians were roughed in at the end
of the war from notes made at home and in France.
The Canadians were very confused - as I was - and, I
think it may be that nobody is at all clear. Individually
bought what they thought correct

Plate 21

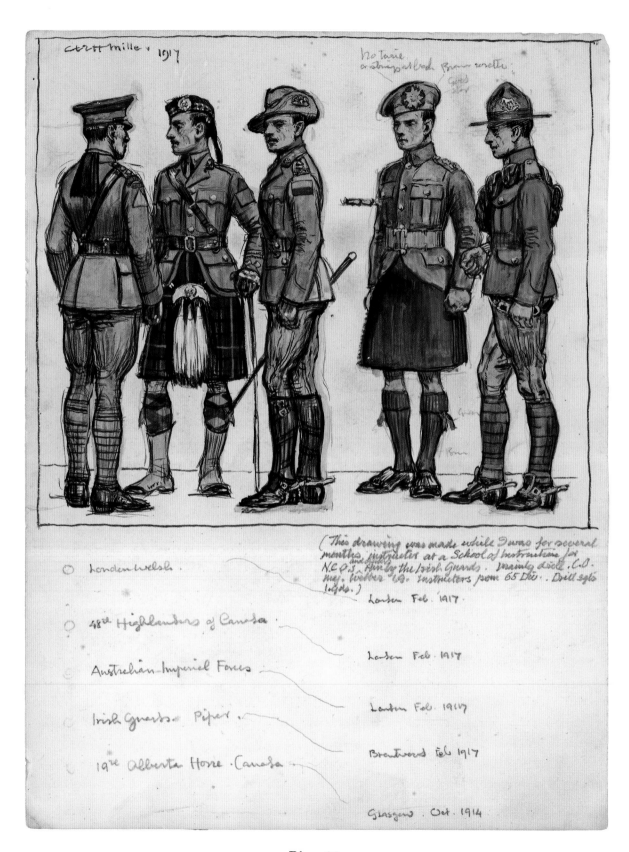

Cecil Miller 1917

No tane
a strap at back. Brown rosette
Gold star

(This drawing was made while I was for several
months, instructor at a School of Instruction for
N.C.O.'s run by the Irish Guards. mainly drill. C.O.
maj. Walker ??. Instructors from 65 Div. Drill sgts
1 Gds.)

○ London Welsh.   London Feb. 1917.

○ 48th Highlanders of Canada.   London Feb. 1917

○ Australian Imperial Forces   London Feb. 1917

○ Irish Guards. Piper.   Brentwood Feb 1917

○ 19th Alberta Horse. Canada   Glasgow. Oct. 1914

Plate 22

CANADA – AVSTRALIA – N.ZEALAND.

○ New Zealand

February 1917 Brentwood.

○ Canada. 72ⁿᵈ Highlanders, Piper(?)   October 1914. Glasgow.

○ Canada. 5ᵗʰ Royal Scots

○ Australia.

Lausen. February 1917.

○ New Zealand. Mounted Rifles (Canterbury?)

Lausen. 1915.

Plate 23

INDIA — SOUTH AFRICA — CANADA.

① Indian Army. Lancers. Captain.

② South Africa. Scottish Battalion. Major (Bim Alfords Guns. Scottish Corp) _London. 1917_

③ Canada. Field Artillery. Gunner. The Green cap band and shoulder straps were worn when the first Canadian forces appeared in France. _London 1916_

④ Indian Army. 58th Vaughans Rifles (Frontier Force.)

⑤ South Africa. Scottish Battalion. Private. _London 1916_

⑥ Canada. 8th Infantry Battalion. Private. British made forelock he wears C on collar. _London 1916_

Brentwood 1917.

Plate 24

Rosette worn by ranks of sergt. & upwards.

Blah

Officers silk bound. Straight tails.

glengarry

Private's glengarry leather bound. Tails crossed.

Badge removed.

Brass titles

Left side only

Both sides.

Stencilled white badge 7 under

PALESTINE nov. 17 - Mar 18

white on khaki

Battn marks on right sleeve only

Normally all uniforms are identical with 2nd Battn

Sergeant 1914 Church parade order.

Lieut 1914 Orderly officer. Special regimental pattern patrol jacket.

Corporal. Order of dress on patrols. FRANCE. marks as worn from JUNE-SEPT. '18 Sacking round bayonet. Cap comforters also worn. Equipment seldom.

Lieut. FRANCE. Marks as amended Oct. '18 Badges worn sometimes polished. Brown boots or puttees. Rank on cuffs or shoulder straps

Private. as in GALLIPOLI '15 and PALESTINE '16-17. Serge issued in winter. Steel helmets and SBRs issued nov. '17

7TH (BLYTHSWOOD) BATTN HIGHLAND LIGHT INFANTRY (TERRITORIAL)
157 BDE. 52 (LOWLAND) DIVN

A. Forbes 1919

Plate 25

THE GERMAN EMPIRE

The uniforms of the German Empire before the First World War were particularly varied and colourful, deriving from the different states that formed the German Empire in 1871, and they had not changed much from that date. The core of the Imperial Army was formed by that of Prussia, which absorbed the troops of most of the minor dukedoms, states and provinces under the federal constitution. The three big exceptions were the kingdoms of Bavaria, Saxony and Württemberg, which retained varying degrees of autonomy in their organisation and uniform.

This led to a somewhat complicated system of regimental titles. Prussian regiments had one number; those of directly affiliated states had a second number in brackets, and only Bavarian units kept their old numbers. Apart from their basic uniforms, the armies of the various states were further distinguished by the different heraldry on their helmet and shako plates, and the state cockades which were worn on the headdress, in conjunction with the red, white and black Reichskokarde. Haswell Miller made a gallant attempt to show these cockades on his figures, but they are not always very clear.

By 1900 Germany had possessions in East and West Africa, Cameroon, Togoland, New Guinea, Samoa, and a foothold in China. The Schutztruppe and police responsible for law and order in these territories wore a variety of clothing inspired by British colonial models, but in grey or a brownish khaki, with much use of corduroy; these are shown in figures 63 and 152–3.

The German Army wore its full-dress uniforms right up to August 1914, when it went into the field-grey service dress which had been introduced in 1910. Prior to 1914 this would not have been seen by a casual observer like Haswell Miller, as it was not permitted to be worn outside barracks except on manoeuvres. (JM)

ORDERS OF DRESS

While German officers had a host of elaborate orders of dress such as 'society or evening dress' and 'gala dress', we do not need to concern ourselves with them here as Haswell Miller does not show any of them. The remainder can be broken down into the five following outfits.

1. Parade dress (Paradenanzug). *As for service dress but with plumes and other full-dress embellishments worn on the headdress.*

2. Service dress (Dienstanzug). *Full dress; headdress without plumes and embellishments.*
3. Undress (Kleinerdienstanzug). *Also walking-out dress. For officers, frock coats, and undress jackets (Litewka Attila and Waffenrock) for those units which had them, with full-dress headdress or forage cap. For other ranks, tunics, full and undress jackets, with forage caps.*
4. Guard order (Wachanzug). *Service dress with pouches for the infantry.*
5. Marching order (Feldanzug). *Service dress with full equipment including packs.*

RANK BADGES

General Officers' rank badges are not included.

Staff officers
Colonel. *Gold or silver fringed epaulettes (for parade), otherwise plaited black and silver cord shoulder straps, both with two lozenge-shaped stars.*
Lieutenant-Colonel. *The same but with one star.*
Major. *The same but without stars.*

Subaltern officers
Captain. *Gold or silver epaulettes without fringe (for parade), and plain black and silver cord shoulder straps, both with two lozenge-shaped stars.*
Lieutenant. *The same but with one star.*
Second Lieutenant. *The same but without stars.*

Non-commissioned officers
Feldwebel. *(.Wachtmeister in mounted units) (Regimental Sergeant-Major). Gold or silver braid edging to collar and cuffs with a large heraldic button; officers' sword knot (portepee).*
Vizefeldwebel. *(Staff Sergeant). As Feldwebel.*
Sergeant. *As Feldwebel but with other ranks' portepee.*
Fahnrich. *(Ensign – Aspirant Officer). As Sergeant but with officers' portepee.*
Unteroffizier. *(Corporal). Braid edging to collar and cuff only, and with other ranks' portepee.*
Gefreiter *(Lance-Corporal). Plain collar, with smaller heraldic button, and other ranks' portepee.*

Einjahriger *(One Year Volunteer). Black and white cord edging to shoulder straps, and other ranks' portepee.*

Plate 26: figures 1–6
Note: place-names in brackets denote the unit's garrison town. (JM)

1. **Bavaria**. Private, *Leib* Regiment [Foot Guards] (Munich), winter marching order.
2. **Prussia** (ex Hesse-Kassel). Band Corporal, 2nd Infantry Regiment (No. 82), undress with forage cap.
3. **Bavaria**. Private, *Leib* Regiment (Munich), undress with forage cap.
4. **Prussia**. Pioneer, Guard Pioneer Battalion (Berlin), parade dress (helmet ball replaced by hair plume).
5. **Bavaria**. Corporal, 2nd Infantry Regiment (Munich), 10th Company of 3rd Battalion, marching order. Battalion and company indicated by colours of bayonet knot.
6. **Saxony**. Pioneer, 2nd Pioneer Battalion (No. 22) (Dresden), 4th Company, marching order.

Plate 27: figures 7–12

7. **Bavaria**. Officer, 8th Light Horse Regiment (Dillingen), undress with frock coat.
8. **Prussia**. Officer, Cuirassier Regiment Emperor Nicholas of Russia (No. 6) (Brandenburg), undress with greatcoat.
9. **Bavaria**. Subaltern Officer, 1st Lancer Regiment (Bamberg), undress with frock coat.
10. **Bavaria**. Officer, 1st Infantry Regiment (Munich), undress cloaked.
11. **Bavaria**. Major-General, undress with frock coat.
12. **Bavaria**. Subaltern Officer, 1st Field Artillery Regiment (Munich), parade dress.

Haswell Miller has included at the bottom of the plate rough sketches of the various cockades used on the headdress. Reading from left to right, they are: the Empire, Prussia, Bavaria (officers), Bavaria, Württemberg, Baden, Hesse, Mecklenburg, Brunswick, Anhalt (entirely green), and Saxony. (JM)

Plate 28: figures 13–23

13. **Bavaria**. Pioneer, 3rd Pioneer Battalion, undress.
14. **Bavaria**. Gunner, 3rd Foot Artillery Regiment, service dress with forage cap.
15. **Bavaria**. NCO, Railway Battalion, service dress with forage cap.
16. **Bavaria**. One Year Volunteer, 2nd Infantry Regiment, undress with greatcoat.
17. **Bavaria**. Corporal, 4th Light Horse Regiment, dismounted service dress.
18. **Bavaria**. Trooper, 2nd Light Horse Regiment, mounted service dress with forage cap.
19. **Bavaria**. Trooper, Staff Corps, service dress with forage cap.
20. **Bavaria**. Private, Medical Troops, undress with forage cap.
21. **Prussia**. Trooper, 1st *Leib* Cuirassier Regiment (Breslau), mounted service dress with forage cap.
22. **Baden**. Gunner, 1st Field Artillery Regiment (No. 14), undress with forage cap.
23. **Bavaria**. Lance-Corporal, 1st Train [Supply] Battalion, mounted service dress.

Plate 29: figures 24–32a

24. **Bavaria**. Private, *Leib* Regiment, undress with forage cap.
25. **Bavaria**. Trooper, 4th Lancer Regiment, service dress with forage cap.
26. **Saxony**. One Year Volunteer, 1st Field Artillery Regiment (No. 12), undress with forage cap.
27. **Bavaria**. Senior NCO, 3rd Light Horse Regiment, undress with issue greatcoat.
28. **Bavaria**. Senior NCO, *Leib* Regiment, undress with private purchase greatcoat.
29. **Bavaria**. Private, Balloon Section of the Engineers, undress with shako.
30. **Bavaria**. Sergeant-Major, Medical Troops, undress with forage cap.
31. **Bavaria**. Private, Medical Corps, service dress.
32. **Württemberg**. Gunner, 2nd Field Regiment (No. 29), undress with forage cap.
32a. **Württemberg**. Trooper, 1st Lancer Regiment (No. 13), undress with forage cap.

This was, I think, the first page of uniform sketches that I made in Munich, settled in my room in Türkenstrasse 57 in August 1908. It is hard to remember how much I knew about what I saw, or how little. I would certainly have known that the Bavarian Army was more independent than any other German state. I think I could begin to guess what each uniform was that I encountered. It was not long before I realised that the *Türkenkaserne*, a couple of blocks down the street towards the city, was the home of the *Infanterie Leib* Regiment. Figure 24 was from here, and probably also the more elegant figure 28, although one cannot see the crown on his shoulder strap and the *Litzen* – white lace bars – on his collar. Why figure 24 carries a short old pattern sword I don't know, but a number of older and less active men seemed to wear these, and I supposed them to be regimentally employed, and not liable to drill and have to fix bayonets. The cap he wears is his peakless working one. The other man has bought his cap and probably everything else visible. He could be any Bavarian infantry regiment and probably is an *Unteroffizier*. The man facing him is an NCO of the 3rd *Chevauleger* Regiment (pink facings and yellow metal buttons). His greatcoat is the issue dark black-grey pattern and the tunic and trousers green.

The second figure is an *Uhlan* of the 4th Regiment, not dressed for walking out. The rather shapeless riding trousers have leather on the inside part. The smart third figure is an *Einjahrager* of Saxon Artillery, unlike nearly all other German artillery who wear blue with black facings. Figure 29 belongs to the Balloon Section of the Engineer Corps and is Bavarian. He and the following two Medical Corps soldiers prove to be Bavarian by wearing blue trousers instead of black-grey, the normal German trouser colouring worn by figures 32 and 32a. Figure 32 belongs to the 2nd Württemberg Field Artillery Regiment (No. 29), Prinz Luitpold von Bayern. Both of these are shown to be Württembergers by the red and black cockade on the cap band. Figure 32a is from the *Uhlan* Regiment.

Plate 30: figures 33–42

All Bavarian except for 34 and 40.

33. Private, 1st *Jäger* [Rifle] Regiment, undress with forage cap.
34. **Prussia**. Sergeant-Major, Guard *Jäger* [Rifles] Regiment, undress with forage cap.
35. Bandsman, 9th Infantry Regiment, undress with forage cap.
36. Private, *Leib* Regiment, undress with helmet.
37. Lance-Corporal, 2nd Lancer Regiment, undress with forage cap.
38. Trooper, 1st Lancer Regiment, service dress with Lancer helmet.
39. Sergeant-Major, *Leib* Regiment, service dress.
40. **Prussia**. Trooper, 1st *Leib* Cuirassier Regiment, undress with working jacket (*Litewka*) and forage cap.
41. Lance-Corporal, 9th Infantry Regiment, undress with forage cap.
42. One Year Volunteer, 2nd Heavy Cavalry Regiment, service dress with forage cap.

Plate 31: figures 43–52

All Bavarian.

43. Trooper, 7th Light Horse Regiment, undress with forage cap.
44. Cadet, *Leib* Regiment, undress with forage cap. The cadets of the Bavarian Military Academy wore the uniforms of their regiments.
45. Gunner, 1st Field Artillery Regiment, undress with forage cap.
46. Bandmaster, 2nd Infantry Regiment, undress with helmet.
47. Lance-Corporal, 1st Field Artillery Regiment, service dress.
48. Field Officer, Field Artillery, undress with frock coat.
49. Subaltern Officer, 1st Infantry Regiment, undress.
50. Trooper, 1st Heavy Cavalry Regiment, service dress.
51. Trooper, 2nd Heavy Cavalry Regiment, undress with forage cap.
52. Officer, Military Justice Department, undress.

Plate 32: figures 53–62

53. **Baden**. Private, 6th Infantry Regiment (No. 114), undress with greatcoat.
54. **Württemberg**. Bandsman, 1st Foot Artillery Regiment (No. 13), undress: back view.
55. **Württemberg**. Bandsman, 1st Foot Artillery Regiment (No. 13), undress: side view.
56. **Prussia**. 1st or 5th Guard Regiment (Instructor, Berlin-Lichterfelde Cadet School), undress.
57. **Bavaria**. Sergeant-Major, Staff Corps, service dress with forage cap.
58. **Bavaria**. Trooper, 1st Train Battalion, mounted service dress with forage cap.
59. **Württemberg**. Lieutenant, 1st Lancer Regiment (No. 19), undress with frock coat.
60. **Saxony**. Trooper, Guard Cavalry Regiment, undress with greatcoat and forage cap.
61. **Baden**. Private, *Leib-Grenadier* Regiment (No. 109), undress with forage cap.
62. **Baden**. Private, 8th Infantry Regiment (No. 169), undress with forage cap.

Plate 33: figures 63–72

63. **German South-West Africa**. Officer, *Schutztruppe*, service dress with home service tunic.
64. **Prussia**. Sergeant-Major, Guard Infantry, undress with greatcoat.

65. **Prussia**. Officer, 2nd Rheinisch Hussar Regiment (No. 9) (Strassburg), parade dress with greatcoat.
66. **Württemberg**. Officer, 1st Lancer Regiment (No. 19), parade dress with greatcoat.
67. **Prussia**. Officer, Dragoon Regiment, parade dress with greatcoat.
68. **Bavaria**. Trooper, 1st Light Horse Regiment, parade dress.
69. **Bavaria**. Trooper, 6th Light Horse Regiment, parade dress.
70. **Bavaria**. Sergeant-Major, 5th Light Horse Regiment, dismounted parade dress.
71. **Bavaria**. Trumpeter, 4th Field Artillery Regiment, parade dress with greatcoat.
72. **Bavaria**. Trooper, 2nd Heavy Cavalry Regiment, parade dress.

Plate 34: figures 73–82

73. **Prussia**. Trooper, Cuirassier Regiment (Rhein) (No. 8) (Cologne-Deutz), undress with working tunic (*Waffenrock*) and forage cap. Seen in Cologne.
74. **Prussia**. Sergeant-Major or Sergeant, Cuirassier Regiment (Rhein) (No. 8) (Cologne-Deutz), undress with *Waffenrock* and forage cap. Seen in Cologne.
75. **Saxony**. Corporal, Field Artillery Regiment (No. 28) (Pirna), undress with forage cap. Seen in Mainz.
76. **Prussia**. Officer, Cuirassier Regiment (Rhein) (No. 8) (Cologne-Deutz), undress with frock coat and forage cap. Seen in Cologne.
77. **Saxony**. Corporal, 2nd *Jäger* Battalion (No. 13) (Dresden), service dress with forage cap. Seen in Munich.
78. **Prussia**. Gunner, 1st Nassau Field Artillery Regiment (Oranian No. 27), undress with helmet. Seen in Mainz and Wiesbaden.
79. **Saxony**. NCO, *Leib-Grenadier* Regiment (No. 100) (Dresden), undress with forage cap.
80. **Prussia**. Private, 1st Foot Guard Regiment (Potsdam), undress with forage cap. Seen in Munich.
81. **Baden**. Private, 3rd Fusilier Battalion, 2nd Grenadier Regiment (No. 110) (Mannheim and Heidelberg), summer parade dress. Seen in Munich.
82. **Prussia**. Sergeant-Major, Guard Train Battalion (Berlin), undress with forage cap. Seen in Mainz.

Plate 35: figures 83–92

83. **Prussia**. Officer, 1st (Rhein) Train Battalion (No. 8), undress with frock coat. Seen in Coblenz.

84. **Prussia**. Captain, Field Artillery, undress with frock coat. Seen in Munich.
85. **Hesse-Darmstadt**. Private, 3rd *Grosherzoglich* Infantry Regiment (*Leibregiment Groshertzogin*) (No. 117), undress with forage cap. Seen in Mainz.
86. **Prussia**. Officer, 2nd *Leib* Hussar Regiment (Danzig-Langfuhr), undress with working tunic (*Attila*) and forage cap. Seen in Munich.
87. **Saxony**. Gunner, 1st Field Artillery Regiment (No. 12) (Metz), marching order. Seen in Würtzburg.
88. **Prussia** (ex Hanover). Band Corporal, 2nd Dragoon Regiment (No. 16) (Lüneberg), undress with forage cap. Seen in Mannheim.
89. **Prussia**. Trooper, 1st Kurhessian Hussar Regiment (No. 13) (Diedenhofen), undress with forage cap. Seen in Munich.
90. **Prussia**. Private, 2nd Nassau Infantry Regiment (No. 88), service dress. Seen in Mainz.
91. **Hesse-Darmstadt**. Private, 4th Infantry Regiment (No. 118) (Worms), summer undress with forage cap. Seen in Mainz.
92. **Prussia**. Private, 1st Silesian Grenadier Regiment (No. 10) (Schweidnitz), undress with forage cap. Seen in Mainz.

Plate 36: figures 93–102

93. **Baden**. Trooper, 20th Dragoon Regiment (Karlsruhe), undress with forage cap.
94. **Baden**. Private, 109th *Leib-Grenadier* Regiment (Karlsruhe), undress with forage cap.
95. **Prussia**. Private, Guard Fusilier Regiment, undress with forage cap. Seen at the Cadet School, Wahlstadt.
96. **Württemberg**. Trooper, 1st Dragoon Regiment (No. 25) (Ludwigsburg), undress with forage cap.
97. **Württemberg**. Trooper, 2nd Lancer Regiment (No. 20) (Ludwigsburg), undress with forage cap.
98. **Württemberg**. Private, 3rd Infantry Regiment (No. 121) (Ludwigsburg), service dress with forage cap.
99. **Prussia**. Second Lieutenant, 1st *Leib* Hussar Regiment (Danzig-Langfuhr), service dress with forage cap.
100. **Saxony**. Corporal, 8th Infantry Regiment (No. 107) (Leipzig), undress with forage cap.
101. **Saxony**. Subaltern Officer, 1st Lancer Regiment (No. 17) (Oschatz), undress with forage cap.
102. **Prussia**. Subaltern Officer, Schleswig-Holstein Lancer Regiment (No. 15) (Saarburg), undress with frock coat and forage cap.

Plate 37: figures 103–115

All Prussian.

103. Trooper, Guard Cuirassier Regiment, undress with *Waffenrock* and forage cap, with 2nd class *Fechtabzeizen* chevrons and signaller's badge.
104. Trooper, *Garde du Corps* Regiment, undress with *Waffenrock*.
105. One Year Volunteer, 3rd Brandenburg Hussar Regiment, undress with *Attila* and forage cap.
106. Trooper, 1st Mounted Rifles Regiment, undress with helmet.
107. Trooper, 1st Mecklenburg Dragoon Regiment (No. 18), undress with forage cap.
108. Bandsman, 5th Mounted Rifles Regiment, service dress.
109. Second Lieutenant, 16th (Schleswig-Holstein) Hussar Regiment, service dress.
110. Bandsman, Telegraph Battalion, service dress with signaller's badge and marksman's lanyard.
111. Drummer, 4th Guard Grenadier Regiment, guard order.
112. Bandsman, Kaiser Alexander Guard Grenadier Regiment, parade dress.
113. Lieutenant, 2nd *Leib* Hussar Regiment, service dress with pelisse.
114. Subaltern Officer, 2nd Guard Grenadier Regiment, parade dress.
115. Subaltern Officer, Guard Fusilier Regiment, parade dress.

Plate 38: figures 116–127

All Prussian except for 126.

116. Subaltern Officer, Magdeburg Hussar Regiment (No. 10) (Stendal), service dress.
117. Standard-bearer (*Fahnentrager*), Foot Guards, service dress with greatcoat. He wears a gorget as a sign of office.
118. Standard-bearer (*Fahnentrager*), 3rd Foot Guard Regiment, parade dress.
119. Subaltern Officer, Hanoverian Hussar Regiment (No. 15) (Wandsbek), winter service dress with pelisse.
120. Captain, 1st Guard Grenadier Regiment, parade dress.
121. Sergeant-Major, 2nd Guard Field Artillery Regiment, undress.
122. Trooper, Life Guard Hussar Regiment (Potsdam), winter service dress with pelisse.
123. Trooper, Life Guard Hussar Regiment (Potsdam), winter service dress with pelisse and forage cap.

124. Trooper, 3rd Guard Lancer Regiment, service dress.
125. Officer, Mounted Rifles, service dress. A Mounted Rifle regiment was attached to each army corps. This regiment, attached to the Guard corps, wore Guards' loops on the collar and cuffs.
126. **Saxony.** Trooper, 3rd Lancer Regiment (No. 21), undress with forage cap.
127. Sergeant-Major, 2nd Silesian Rifle Battalion (No. 6), parade dress.

Plate 39: figures 128–138

All Prussian.

128. NCO, 5th Foot Guard Regiment, undress with greatcoat and forage cap.
129. Drummer, 4th Foot Guard Regiment, parade dress.
130. Bandmaster, 2nd Foot Guard Regiment, parade dress.
131. One Year Volunteer, 3rd Foot Guard Regiment, service dress with greatcoat.
132. *Fahnentrager*, 2nd Foot Guard Regiment, guard order.
133. Private, Guard *Schützen* Battalion, service dress. The Guard *Schützen* had black 'Swedish' cuffs (with pointed flaps) and collars, with yellow braid loops (*Litzen*).
134. Trooper, 1st Guard Dragoon Regiment, undress with helmet.
135. Trooper, 2nd Westphalian Hussar Regiment (No. 11), service dress with forage cap.
136. Trooper, 17th Brunswick Hussar Regiment, service dress with forage cap.
137. Trooper, 2nd Guard Cuirassier Regiment, undress with *Waffenrock* and forage cap.
138. Trooper, Oldenburg Dragoon Regiment (No. 19), service dress with forage cap.

Plate 40: figures 139–149

All Prussian.

139. Second Lieutenant, 4th Guard Grenadier Regiment, undress with helmet.
140. Officer, Guard Cuirassier Regiment, undress with greatcoat and forage cap.
141. Second Lieutenant, Guard Hussar Regiment, service dress with greatcoat.
142. Private, Fusilier Battalion, 2nd Guard Grenadier Regiment, drill order.
143. Band Sergeant, 2nd Foot Guard Regiment, undress with helmet.
144. Trooper, 1st Silesian Hussar Regiment (No. 4), service dress with forage cap.

145. Private, 3rd Guard Grenadier Regiment, marching order with marksman's lanyard.

146. Second Lieutenant, 4th Foot Guard Regiment, undress with helmet.

147. Trooper, 2nd Mounted Rifles Regiment, service dress with forage cap.

148. Lance-Corporal, 3rd Foot Guard Regiment, parade dress.

149. Subaltern Officer, 1st Pomeranian Lancer Regiment (No. 4), undress with forage cap.

Plate 41: figures 150–164

(Note: Haswell Miller's numbering has gone astray here.)

150. **Prussia**. Trumpeter, 1st Guard Field Artillery Regiment, parade dress.

151. **Prussia**. Bandsman, 1st Guard Field Artillery Regiment, parade dress with greatcoat.

152. **German East Africa**. Subaltern Officer, *Schutztruppe*, walking-out dress with home *Waffenrock* and forage cap.

153. **German West Africa**. Subaltern Officer, Togoland and Cameroon *Schutztruppe*, walking-out dress with home *Waffenrock* and forage cap.

154. **Prussia**. Subaltern Officer, Guard *Jäger* Battalion, parade dress. The Guard Jäger had red 'Brandenburg' (round) cuffs and collars, with yellow braid loops (*Litzen*).

155. **Prussia**. Subaltern Officer, 2nd Guard Field Artillery Regiment, parade dress.

156. **Saxony**. Subaltern Officer, Rifle Battalion No. 13, parade dress.

157. **Saxony**. Subaltern Officer, 2nd Lancer Regiment (No. 18), parade dress.

158. **Prussia**. Subaltern Officer, Guard Fusilier Regiment, parade dress.

159. **Saxony**. Private, Rifle Regiment (No. 108), parade dress.

160. **Prussia**. Trooper, 6th Mounted Rifles Regiment, attached to XIth Army Corps, mounted service dress with forage cap. Mounted Rifle regiments bore on their shoulder straps the number of the army corps to which they were attached.

161. **Saxony**. Subaltern Officer, 2nd Heavy Cavalry Regiment (Carabiniers), undress with helmet.

GERMANY

① "Infanterie-Leib-Regiment" Bavaria, Munich. Private. (Bavarian Foot-Guard Reg.)

② "2 Kurhessisches Infanterie Regiment No. 82" Göttingen, "Unteroffizier" of band. Walking out dress. Rank shown by gold binding on collar and sleeve.

③ "(Bayer) Infanterie-Leib-Regiment. Munich. Private.

④ "Garde-Pionier-Bataillon" Prussia. Berlin, "Pionier" Review Order (Pioneer Batt. of the Guard)

⑤ "2 (Bayer) Infanterie Regiment "Kronpring" Munich. "Gefreiter" of 10th Company. 3rd Battalion.
    Rank shown by button on collar. Company indicated by coloured sword knot. Marching order

⑥ "Königl. Sachsische Pionier-Bataillon No. 12" Dresden. "Pionier" of 4th Company, Marching
    order. (Royal Saxon Pioneer Batt.)

Plate 26

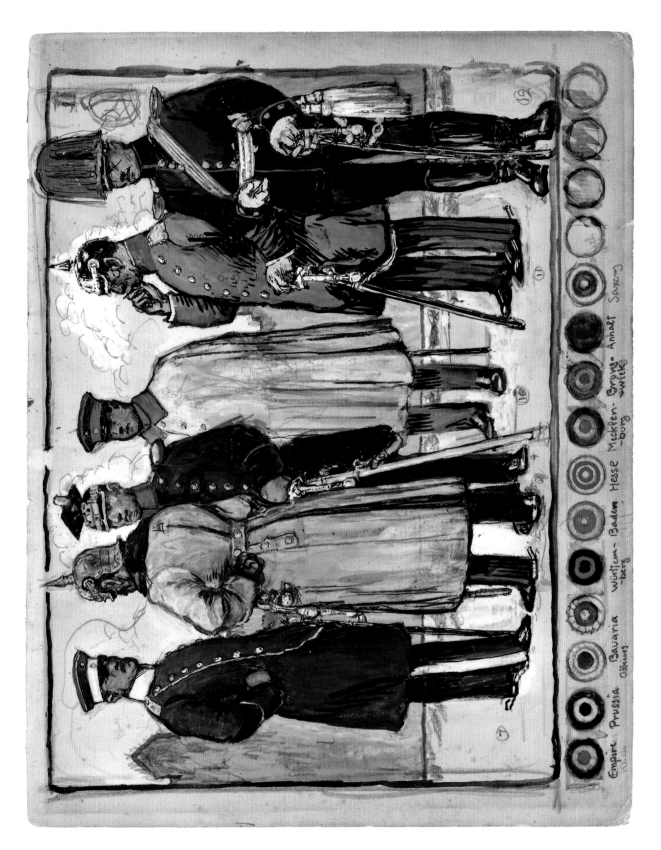

Plate 27

Plate 28

Sept. 1908 GERMANY IV

Infanterie Leib Regiment

Infanterie Reg

3 Chevaulegers Regt

Luftschiff Abteilung

Plate 29

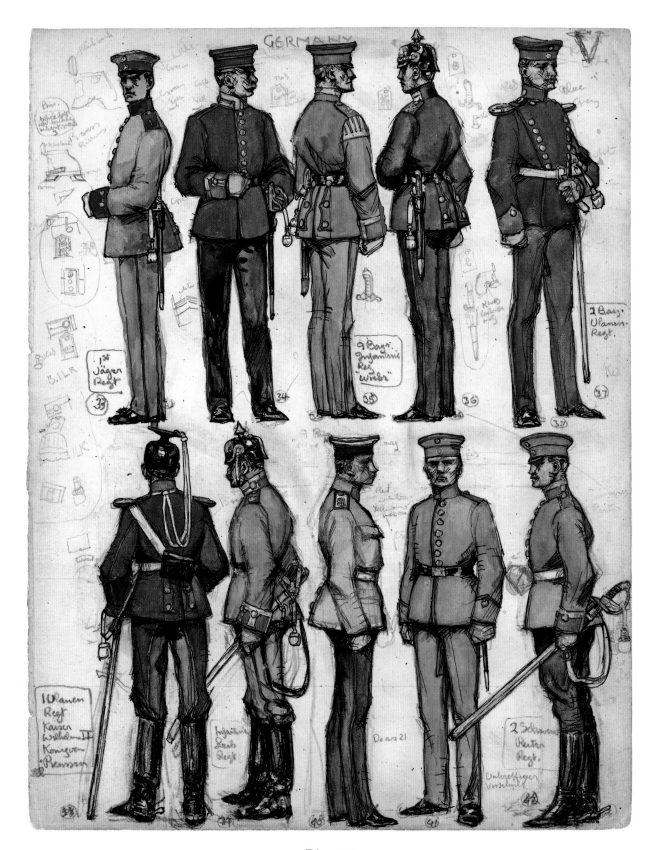

Plate 30

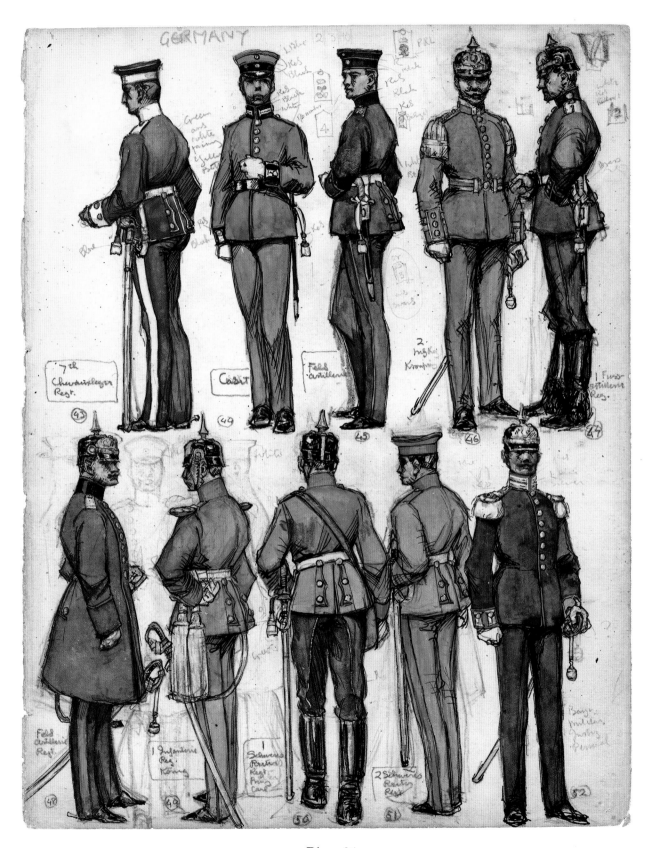

GERMANY

Plate 31

Plate 32

Plate 33

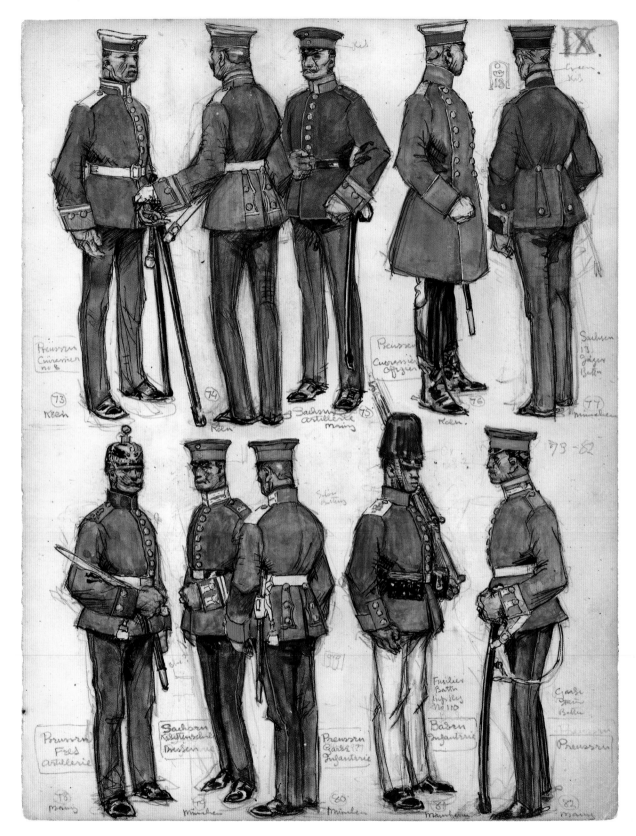

Plate 34

Plate 35

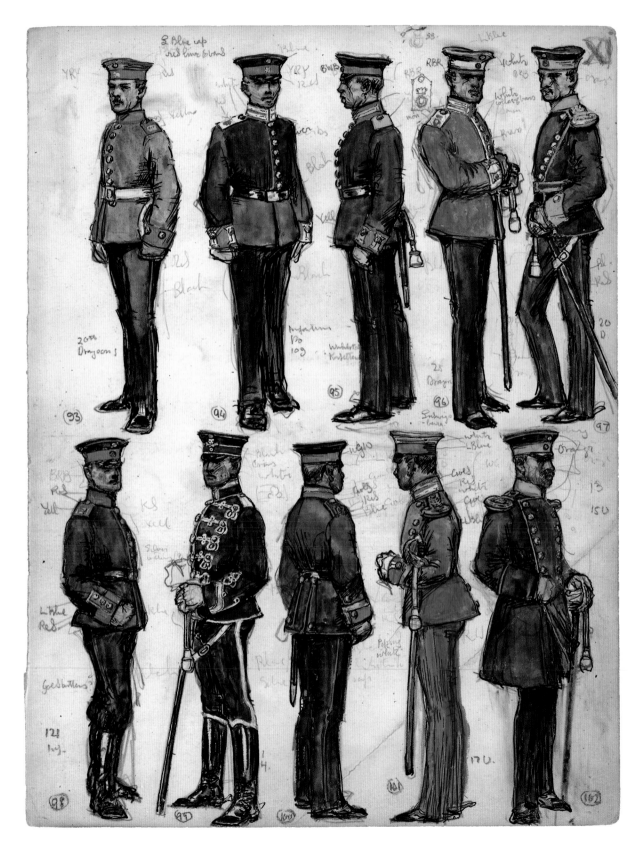

Plate 36

Plate 37

Plate 38

Plate 39

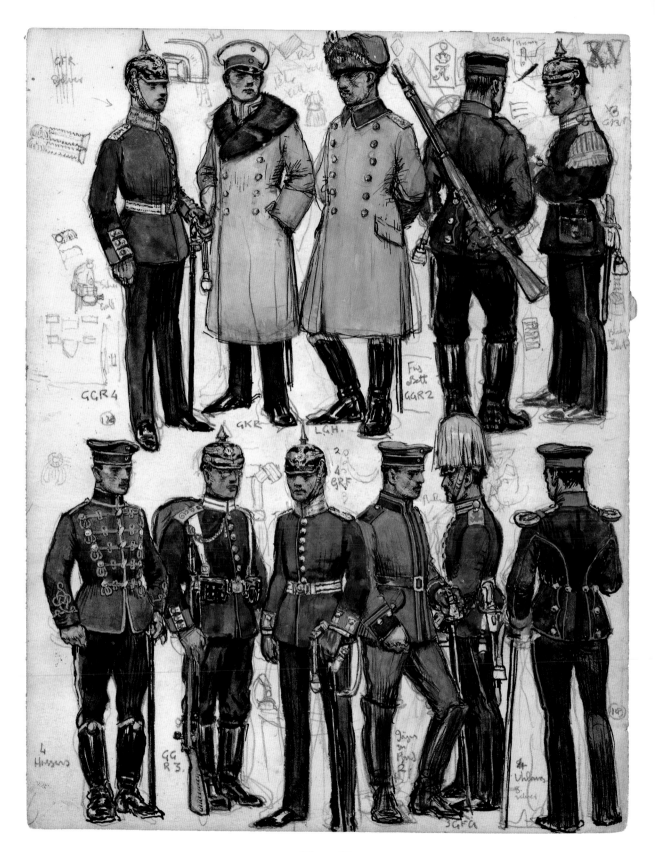

Plate 40

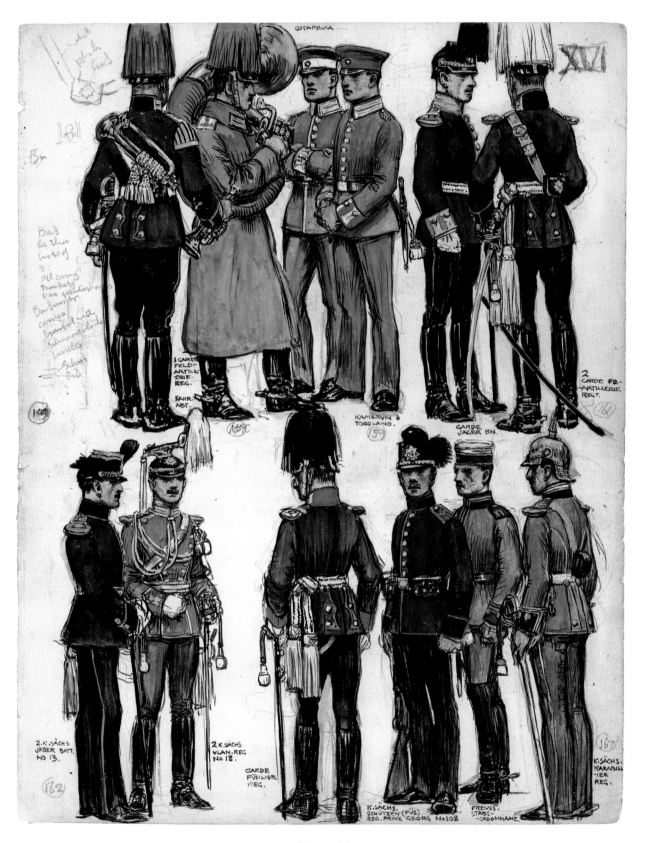

OSTAFRIKA

XVI

1 GARDE
FELD-
ARTILLE
RIE
REG.

FAHR.
ABT.

KAMERUN
TOGOLAND.

GARDE
JÄGER BN.

2
GARDE FD.-
ARTILLERIE
REGT.

2.K.SÄCHS
JÄGER BATT.
NO 13.

2 K.SÄCHS.
ULAN.REG.
No 18.

GARDE
FÜSILIER
REG.

K.SÄCHS.
SCHÜTZEN (FÜS)
REG. PRINZ GEORG No 108

PREUSS.
STABS
-ORDONNANZ

K.SÄCHS.
KARABIN
-IER
REG.

Plate 41

FRANCE

Following the introduction of a khaki service dress by the British in 1902, and field-grey by the Germans in 1910, the French began a series of trials of a new service dress in 1910. Earlier attempts, notably in 1903 and 1906, had for a variety of reasons come to nothing. The proposed new uniforms were in a greenish-grey colour called reseda, and consisted of a somewhat curious cloth-covered helmet, a tunic with a turned-down collar, trousers and puttees. Haswell Miller shows this trial uniform in figure 41, giving the colour as a lightish khaki, not unlike that of the British khaki drill. The Minister of War, Berteaux, the main supporter of the new uniforms, was unfortunately killed in an air crash in May 1911, just before they were tried out at the grand manoeuvres of that year. As a result, the numerous critics had a free rein and the scheme came to nothing. His successor, Messimy, set up a new commission, which included the celebrated military artists Édouard Detaille and Georges Scott. This time the red trousers were retained, but light blue as well as dark blue tunics were tried out, together with an elaborate metal helmet designed by Detaille (see figures 10 and 42–3). Three companies of the 28th Infantry paraded in this new tenue on 14 July 1912, but again it met with opposition in many quarters and was not accepted, although it was subsequently used by the 3rd Battery of Horse Artillery. The conservatives had won the day, and the French army marched off in 1914 in all the glory of their pre-war uniforms; it was only in 1915 that they were provided with the celebrated 'horizon' blue service dress and steel helmet. (JM)

ORDERS OF DRESS

1. Parade dress (grande tenue). *Full dress with all possible embellishments on the headdress.*
2. Service dress (petite tenue). *Full dress with plain headdress.*
3. Undress. *Service dress with undress forage cap (képi).*
4. Guard order. *Service dress with belt and pouches.*
5. Marching order (tenue de campagne). *Service dress with full equipment and backpack.*

RANK BADGES

Staff officers
Colonel. *Six rows of gold or silver lace round the cuffs and base of the képi, with three rows crossing the crown of the képi. Two fringed epaulettes.*

Lieutenant-Colonel. *Five rows of gold or silver lace round the cuffs and base of the képi; three rows over the képi. Two fringed epaulettes.*

Major. *Four rows of gold or silver lace round the cuffs and base of the képi; three rows over the képi. Right epaulette without fringe.*

Subaltern officers
Captain. *Three rows of gold or silver lace round the cuffs and base of the képi; two rows over the képi. Two epaulettes with narrow fringe.*

Lieutenant. *Two rows of gold or silver lace round the cuffs and base of the képi; one row over the képi. Right epaulette without fringe.*

Second Lieutenant. *One row of gold or silver lace round the cuffs and base of the képi; one row over the képi. Left epaulette without fringe.*

Non-commissioned officers
Adjudant. *Inverted chevron of gold cord above both cuffs of tunic and greatcoat.*

Sergeant-Major. *Two gold or silver inverted chevrons above both cuffs of the tunic and two diagonal stripes on the greatcoat.*

Sergeant. *One gold or silver inverted chevron above both cuffs of the tunic and one diagonal stripe on the greatcoat.*

Brigadier (Corporal). *Two red inverted chevrons above both cuffs of the tunic and greatcoat.*

Private 1st Class. *One red inverted chevron above both cuffs of the tunic and greatcoat.*

Sous-officier Rengagé. *An NCO who has voluntarily re-enlisted at the end of his service. Coloured piping round tunic and greatcoat cuffs. (JM)*

Plate 42: figures 1–6

1. Trooper, Hussars, parade dress. Light blue piping on breeches is missing.
2. NCO, Artillery, service dress. Probably an Adjudant-chef.
3. Private, Colonial Infantry, service dress with the 1873 pattern tunic.
4. Private, 10th Infantry of the Line (Auxonne), guard order.
5. Brigadier (re-enlisted), Dragoons, parade dress.
6. Officer, Spahis, drill order.

Plate 43: figures 6a–15

6a. Private, Zouaves, service dress.
7. General Staff Secretary, Recruiting Service, service dress.
8. Private, Republican Foot Guards, parade dress.
9. Trooper, Remount Service, service dress.
10. Gunner, Horse Artillery, parade dress with 1902 experimental helmet.
11. Trooper, *Chasseurs à Cheval*, drill order.
12. NCO, *Chasseurs d'Afrique*, undress.
13. Trooper, Dragoons, parade dress.
14. Gunner, Artillery, service dress.
15. European Sergeant, Spahis, service dress.

Plate 44: figures 16–25

16. Private, Republican Foot Guards, walking-out dress.
17. Trooper, 24th Dragoon Regiment, parade dress.
18. Sergeant, *Chasseurs à Cheval*, service dress.
19. Drummer, 107th Infantry of the Line (Angoulême), guard order with greatcoat.
20. Trooper, *Chasseurs d'Afrique*, service dress.
21. Lieutenant, Infantry of the Line, parade dress.
22. Adjudant, 8th Cuirassier Regiment, service dress with képi.
23. Sergeant, 22nd Dragoon Regiment, undress with tunic and képi.
24. Sergeant (Re-enlisted), 24th Section of Medical Troops, service dress with greatcoat and képi.
25. Sergeant (Re-enlisted), 21st *Chasseurs à Pied*, service dress with greatcoat with marksman's badge on left arm.

Plate 45: figures 26–35

26. Trooper, Republican Mounted Guards, dismounted guard order.
27. Sergeant, Republican Foot Guards, guard order with greatcoat.
28. Adjudant, Dragoons, service dress with greatcoat.
29. Sergeant (Re-enlisted), 29th Infantry of the Line (Autun), service dress.
30. Private, Infantry of the Line, guard order with greatcoat.
31. Trooper, 2nd Cuirassier Regiment, service dress with tunic.
30. Corporal, 12th Artillery Regiment, undress.
31. Trooper, Republican Mounted Guards, parade dress.
32. Drummer, Republican Foot Guards, guard order.
33. Private, Republican Foot Guards, guard order.

Plate 46: figures 36–45

36. Private, *Tirailleurs Algériens*, service dress.
37. Sergeant, Hussars, parade dress, with marksman's and swordsman's proficiency badges.
38. Trooper, 5th Cuirassier Regiment, service dress.
39. Zouave, 1st Zouave Regiment, full dress.
40. Trooper, *Chasseurs à Cheval*, service dress.
41. Private, 26th Infantry of the Line, 1911 experimental reseda service dress with greatcoat. The colour here is too beige and should be a lightish grey-green.
42. Infantryman in greatcoat wearing the 1912 experimental Detaille helmet and uniform.
43. Back view of the same.
44. Trooper, 5th Hussars (Nancy), service dress with tunic.
45. Private 1st Class (Re-enlisted), 22nd Colonial Infantry, service dress with greatcoat.

Plate 47: figures 46–55

46. Trooper, Cuirassiers, undress with képi.
47. Officer, 1st Cuirassier Regiment, parade dress. The breeches should have a wide black stripe down the side.
48. Sergeant, *Régiment de Sapeurs Pompiers de la Ville de Paris*, service dress.
49. Private, 126th Infantry of the Line (Brive), guard order with greatcoat. This soldier wears puttees, which were worn only by regiments located in mountain areas.
50. Officer Cadet, St Cyr Military Academy, parade dress.
51. Second Lieutenant, *Chasseurs d'Afrique*, service dress.
52. Sergeant-Major, Republican Foot Guards, service dress with cocked hat.
53. Trumpeter, Republican Foot Guards, guard order.
54. Officer, Infantry of the Line, service dress with cloak.
55. Private, Infantry of the Line, marching order.

Plate 48: figures 56–66

56. Sergeant-Major, 12th Dragoon Regiment, service dress.
57. Trooper, Republican Mounted Guards, undress.
58. Sergeant-Major, 23rd *Chasseurs d'Alpin* (Grasse), undress.
59. NCO, *Régiment de Sapeurs Pompiers de la Ville de Paris*, service dress with frock coat.
60. Spahi, service dress. The headdress should have black cords not orange, the jacket red with black braid, and the waistcoat light blue.
61. Lieutenant, *Tirailleurs Algériens*, service dress.

62. Captain, 2nd *Chasseurs à Pied*, undress.
63. Captain, *Chasseurs à Cheval*, service dress with pelisse.
64. Lieutenant, Horse Artillery, service dress with pelisse.
65. Lieutenant, Infantry of the Line, service dress with pelisse.
66. Captain, Colonial Infantry, service dress with pelisse.

Plate 49: figures 67–77

67. Trooper, Remount Service, service dress.
68. Private, Aeroplane Company of the Engineers, marching order.
69. Administrative Officer, parade dress.
70. Lieutenant, Infantry of the Line, service dress.
71. Lieutenant, Telegraph Section, parade dress. These were not regular soldiers but civil employees.
72. Sergeant-Major, *Chasseurs d'Afrique*, service dress.
73. Sergeant, 4th *Tirailleurs Algériens*, service dress.
74. Sergeant, 3rd Zouave Regiment, service dress.
75. Sergeant, Medical Troops, service dress with greatcoat.
76. Sergeant-Major, 2nd Regiment, Foreign Legion, service dress with greatcoat.
77. Corporal, Foreign Legion, service dress with greatcoat.

Plate 42

Plate 43

Plate 44

Plate 45

Plate 46

Plate 47

Plate 48

Plate 49

AUSTRIA-HUNGARY

Although the Austrian-Hungarian Army has a history that is mainly a distressing tale of defeats, these misfortunes failed to upset the general set-up until the final disaster of 1919. Up to then the Austrians shared with Britain and Spain continuous histories and regimental titles that went back to the beginning of the eighteenth century. Traces of Austrian character remained in the uniforms of German States – for instance Brunswick and Hanover. Although an Empire and a Kingdom there were no 'Guard' Corps as in the German, Russian and even British armies. There were, however, small 'Palace' and 'Crown' Guard units with duties in Vienna and Budapest. Uniforms, for mounted and dismounted, were distinctly contemporary and military, while the Hungarian corps consisted of rather antique hussars and halberdiers.

The Infantry of the Line regiments were not separated into the two monarchies but were mixed quite arbitrarily, only adding *Deutsch* or *Ung* to the numerical titles. They were, however, thoroughly differentiated in uniform in that the Hungarian tunic cuffs had a curious white lace bar with a fringe, and the trousers were light blue 'tights' with yellow and black braid ornaments. Further identification was provided by a scheme of coloured facings combined with a play of white or yellow metal buttons. The colours, however, were rather unsatisfactory: too many greens, greys with extremely delicate variations and odd names. The cavalry consisted of Dragoons (Austrian), Hussars (Hungarian) and Lancers (Polish), and younger 'national' infantry and cavalry which were Bosnian-Herzegovinian and Dalmatian.

The long-standing Landwehr, a territorial defence force based on the militia principle, was reorganised in 1869, as a counterbalance to the Hungarian version, the Honved, *formed two years earlier. In 1887 they became a reserve army of all branches, with the same training and conscription as the regular army, but bound more to the provinces.*

*The Austrian Army could with justification take credit for an early attempt at providing a service dress, when it introduced the undress jacket (*Bluse*) and field cap in the early 1880s, but it was slow to follow this development to its logical conclusion. It was not until 1909 that a pike-grey (*Hechtgrau*) uniform began to be issued to all foot units as well as machine-gun battalions, artillery and the Mounted Tyrolean and Dalmatian Rifles, in which they entered the*

First World War. A projected service dress for the cavalry was also put in hand but was set aside owing to pressure brought to bear on the Emperor, and, like the French, they went to war in all the glory of their traditional full dress. However they were quickly given grey covers for their helmets, and grey trousers, tunics and pelisses. (JM)

ORDERS OF DRESS

As they are in general so similar I have reduced the orders of dress of the remaining countries to the following seven, and have used them throughout, with the occasional added description such as 'mounted' or 'dismounted', 'summer' or 'winter'. As before, General Officers' rank badges (except for the Russians) are not included. (JM)

1. Parade dress. *The best of everything, that is, service dress with all the full dress appointments.*
2. Service dress. *The normal everyday dress, as for parade dress but without the full dress appointments.*
3. Undress. *Usually described as 'service dress' with a variety of undress headwear, tunics or jackets.*
4. Walking-out dress. *As undress but usually without side arms, except in some armies for officers.*
5. Drill order. *Service dress or undress with the minimum of weapons and equipment required to perform the exercise.*
6. Guard order. *Service dress with weapons and ammunition, and other light equipment required for time spent in the guardroom.*
7. Marching order. *Service dress with full equipment.*

RANK BADGES

Staff officers
Colonel. *Lace edging to collar and cuffs and three stars in the reverse of the lace colour.*
Lieutenant-Colonel. *Lace edging to collar and cuffs and two stars, all in the reverse of the lace colour.*
Major. *Lace edging to collar and cuffs and one star in the reverse of the lace colour.*

Subaltern officers
Captain. *Three gold or silver stars on the collar.*

Lieutenant. *Two gold or silver stars on the collar.*
Second Lieutenant. *One gold or silver star on the collar.*

Non-commissioned officers

Aspirant Officers. *Narrower gold lace edging to collar and one silver star.*
Sergeant-Major. *Narrower gold lace edging to collar and one white star.*
Sergeant. *Three white stars on the collar.*
Corporal. *Two white stars on the collar.*
Private 1st Class. *One white star on the collar.*
Einjähriger (One Year Volunteer). *Two rows of yellow braid round the cuffs.*

Plate 50: figures 1–8

1. Sergeant, Gendarmes, service dress.
2. As above.
3. Second Lieutenant, *Tiroler Kaiserjäger*, service dress.
4. As above.
5. Officer, German Infantry Regiment No. 27, parade dress with greatcoat.
6. Captain, Gendarmes, service dress with working tunic (*Bluse*).
7. Officer, *Tyroler Landwehr Landesschützen*, service dress. Although Landwehr, this unit was considered to be an élite corps.
8. Haswell Miller noted this figure as not being Austrian, and suggested he could be Romanian, Swedish or Greek. The general opinion is that he is probably a Romanian officer.

Plate 51: figures 9–16

9. Lieutenant, German Infantry Regiment No. 40, service dress with greatcoat. Back of greatcoat as in figure 5. Seen in Munich.
10. Official, *Pionierzeugesen* (Engineers' Park), summer service dress.
11. Officer, 14th Dragoons, winter service dress with pelisse. Seen in Munich.
12. Lieutenant, Artillery, service dress. Seen in Bozen.
13. Military Intendant (civilian official), service dress.
14. Second Lieutenant, German Infantry Regiment No. 40, summer service dress. Seen in Bozen.
15. Trooper, 12th Dragoons, undress with forage cap. Seen in Bozen.
16. Artillery NCO, service dress with long service chevrons and forage cap. Seen in Riva.

Plate 52: figures 17–24

17. Officer, *Militärkanzlei* (Military Clerks' Office), service dress. Seen in Bozen.
18. Trooper, 6th Dragoons, service dress with forage cap. Seen in Bozen.
19. Lieutenant, Hungarian Infantry Regiment No. 79, summer service dress. Seen in Bozen.
20. Second Lieutenant, *Rechnungsführer* (Invoice Department), service dress with *Bluse*. Seen in Bozen.
21. Private, German Infantry Regiment No. 45, guard order. Seen in Salzburg.
22. Sergeant-Major, *Landsschutzen* Regiment (Bozen) No. 2, service dress with long-service chevrons Seen in Bozen.
23. Private, *Landsschutzen* Regiment (Bozen) No. 2, service dress with marksman's lanyard. Seen on guard in Riva.
24. Sergeant-Major, German Infantry Regiment No. 73, undress with *Bluse* and forage cap.

Plate 53: figures 25–34

25. Sergeant, Artillery, undress with *Bluse* and forage cap. Seen from a train window.
26. Infantry Private, guard order, with the 1909 'pike-grey' service dress.
27. Sergeant, German Infantry Regiment No. 27, service dress with forage cap and marksman's lanyard.
28. Official, 3rd Class, Military Geographcal Institute, service dress.
29. Officer, German *Landwehrschützen*, summer service dress.
30. Second Lieutenant, *Jäger* Regiment No. 4, service dress (with edelweiss on collar).
31. Second Lieutenant, Horse Artillery, mounted service dress.
32. Officer, Train, service dress.
33. Trooper, 9th Dragoons, service dress with forage cap.
34. *Einjahrige*, *Jäger* Regiment No. 4, 1909 pattern service dress (with edelweiss on collar).

Plate 54: figures 35–44

35. Sergeant-Major, German Infantry Regiment No. 18, service dress with forage cap. Seen in Munich.
36. Private 1st Class, German Infantry Regiment No. 45, guard order. Seen on guard in Salzburg.
37. Sergeant-Major, 5th Lancers, service dress with forage cap. Seen in Salzburg.

38. Corporal, Horse Artillery, parade dress.
39. Sergeant-Major, German Infantry Regiment No. 59, parade dress with long-service chevrons.
40. Second Lieutenant, *Jäger*, service dress. Seen in Salzburg.
41. Lieutenant, *Jäger*, service dress.
42. Officer, German Infantry Regiment No. 59, service dress with greatcoat and waterproof cover to shako. Seen in Salzburg.
43. *Einjahrige* (University Graduate), *Jäger*, service dress with forage cap. Seen in Salzburg.
44. Private, German Infantry Regiment No. 43, in 1909 marching order with blue *Bluse* and marksman's lanyard.

Plate 55: figures 45–50

45. Trooper, 3rd Hussars, parade dress.
46. Sergeant, Train, service dress.
47. Private, Bosnia-Herzegovinian Infantry, 1909 pattern marching order.
48. Trooper, *Honved* Hussars, winter service dress with forage cap.
49. Captain, 5th, 9th, 11th & 13th Hussars, service dress with shako.
50. NCO, Artillery, service dress with 1909 pattern greatcoat and forage cap.

Plate 56: figures 53–65

All seen in Vienna in 1913.
53. NCO Trumpeter (*Stabstrompeter*), Artillery, parade dress with greatcoat.
54. Trumpeter, Horse Artillery, parade dress with greatcoat.
55. Private, Hungarian Infantry Regiment No. 41, service dress with marksman's lanyard and forage cap.
56. Life Guard Cavalry Squadron (all ranks of which were officers), undress with *Felberkurtka*, an unofficial but very popular garment among cavalry officers. The *Felber* is an artificial fur dyed red.
57. Officer, Hussars, winter service dress.
58. Infantry Officer, winter service dress.
59. Officer, 15th Hussars, parade dress.
60. Officer, Hussars, service dress with undress shako.
61. Officer, 2nd Dragoons, winter service dress.
62. Officer, 11th Dragoons or 6th or 13th Lancers, winter service dress.
63. Officer, Engineers, winter service dress.
64. Lieutenant, *Honved* Infantry, service dress.
65. Officer, 11th Lancers, winter service dress.

Plate 57: figures 66–78

66. Trooper, Lancers, winter service dress with forage cap. The yellow fringe (*Wasserfall*) at the waist identifies him as a Lancer.
67. Corporal, 5th, 9th, 11th or 13th Hussars, service dress with two proficiency badges on his right breast and forage cap.
68. Private, *Tiroler Kaiserjäger*, guard order with greatcoat.
69. Private, Bosnia-Herzegovena Infantry, winter marching order with marksman's lanyard.
70. Drum Major, Hungarian Infantry Regiment No. 16, parade dress.
71. Private, German Infantry Regiment No. 86, service dress. There is a query as to why he is carrying a sabre.
72. Gunner, Artillery, winter service dress with 1909 pattern greatcoat with marksman's lanyard and forage cap.
73. Trooper, 4th, 7th, 12th or 16th Hussars, service dress with forage cap.
74. Gunner, Artillery, service dress with marksman's lanyard.
75. Farrier, Horse Artillery, service dress.
76. Trooper, 7th Dragoons, winter service dress.
77. Acting Assistant-Surgeon (One Year Volunteer), Medical Troops, service dress.
78. Sergeant-Major (Lieutenant in the Army), Life Guard Cavalry Squadron, parade dress.

Plate 58: figures 79–89

79. Lieutenant, 4th Hussars, dismounted service dress.
80. Officer, German Infantry Regiment No. 94, parade dress.
81. Lieutenant, 6th Lancers, service dress with undress tunic.
82. NCO, 8th Lancers, dismounted service dress with forage cap.
83. Corporal (Sergeant-Major in the Army), Life Guard Infantry Company, parade dress.
84. Medical Officer, *Honved* Medical Troops, parade dress.
85. Officer, *Jäger*, parade dress.
86. Life Guard Cavalry Squadron, undress with *Felberkurtka* as figure 56.
87. Official, Border Administration Department, Hungarian Section, service dress.
88. Bugler, *Kaiserjäger*, 1909 service dress.
89. Drummer, Hungarian Infantry Regiment No. 16, marching order.

Plate 59: figures 90–97

90. Bugler, *Kaiserjäger*, 1909 service dress.
91. Bosnia-Herzegovinian Infantryman, undress.
92. Trooper, 4th Dragoons, service dress with horsemanship proficiency badge on right breast. The collar and cuffs should be a lighter shade of green.
93. Trumpeter, Horse Artillery, parade dress with horsemanship proficiency badge on the right breast.
94. Officer, 3rd Hussars, winter service dress.
95. Lieutenant, 6th Lancers, parade dress with cloak.
96. Officer, German Infantry Regiment No. 40, parade dress.
97. Life Guard Cavalry Squadron, undress with *Felberkurtka* as figures 56 and 86.

Plate 50

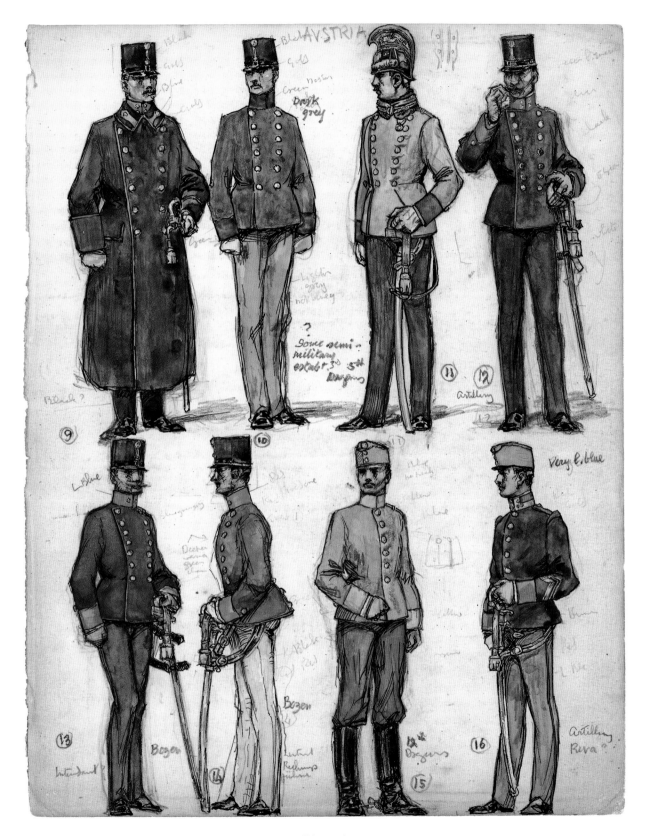

Plate 51

Plate 52

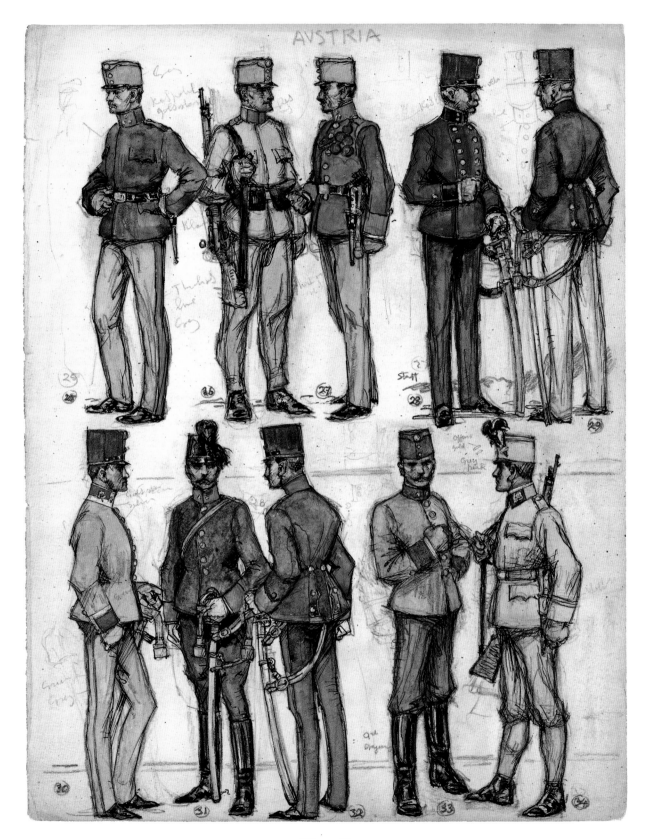

Plate 53

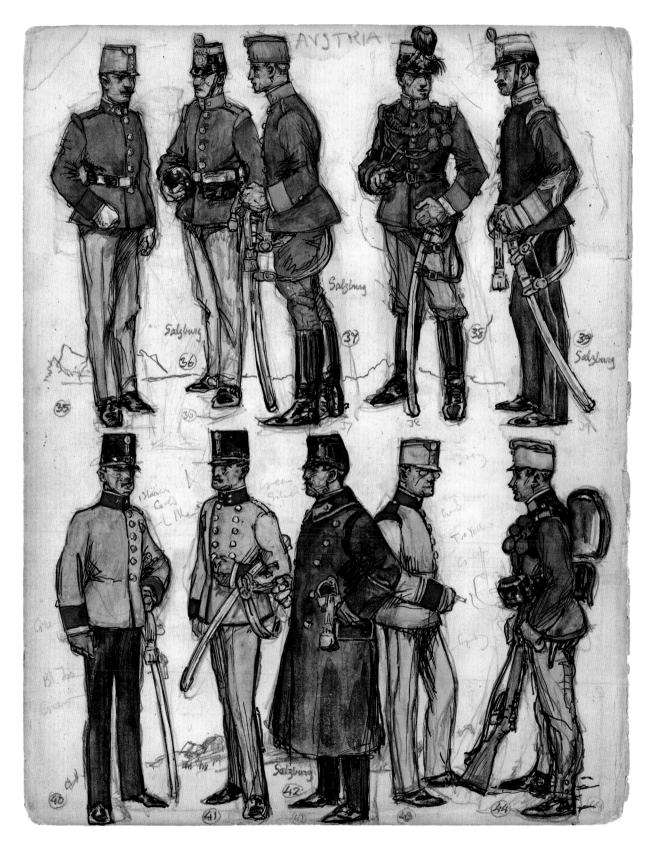

AVSTRIA

Salzburg

Salzburg

Salzburg

Salzburg

Plate 54

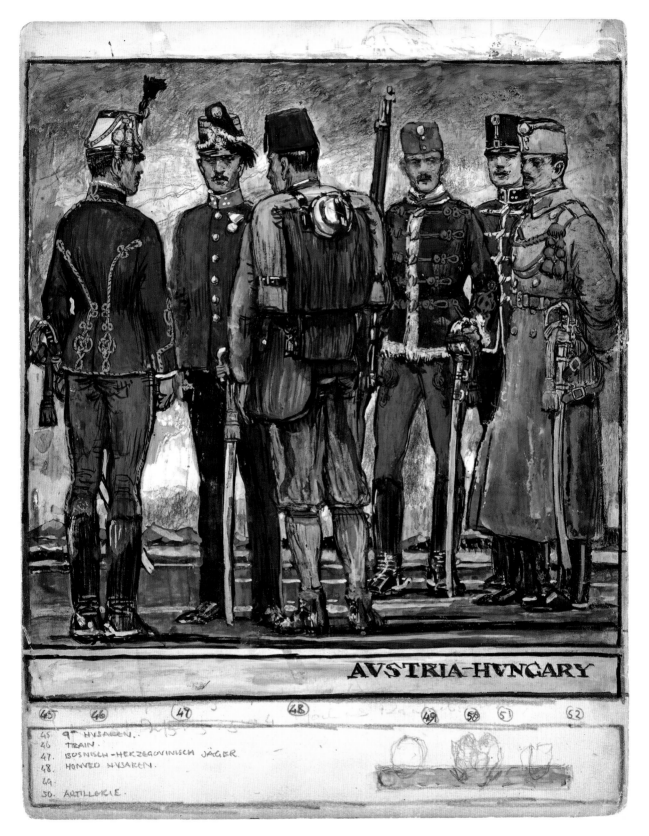

AVSTRIA-HVNGARY

45   46   47   48   49   50   51   52

45. 9ᵀᴴ HVSAREN.
46. TRAIN.
47. BOSNISCH-HERZEGOVINISCH JÄGER.
48. HONVED HVSAREN.
49.
50. ARTILLERIE.

Plate 55

Plate 56

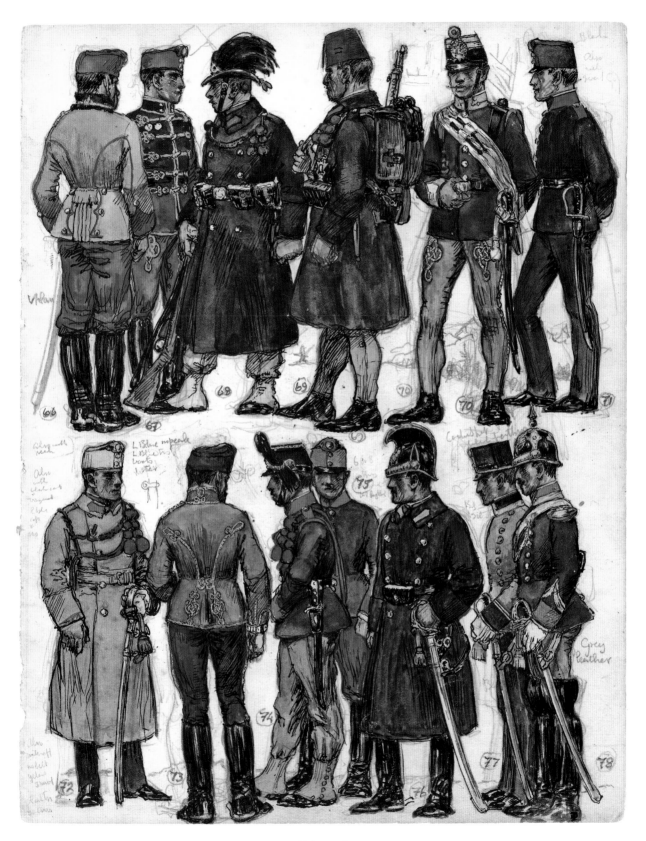

Plate 57

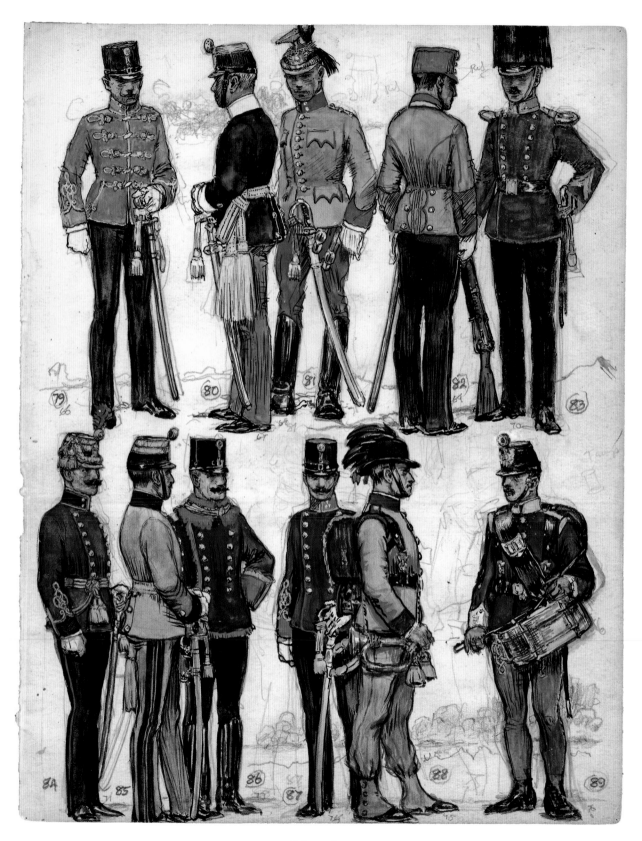

Plate 58

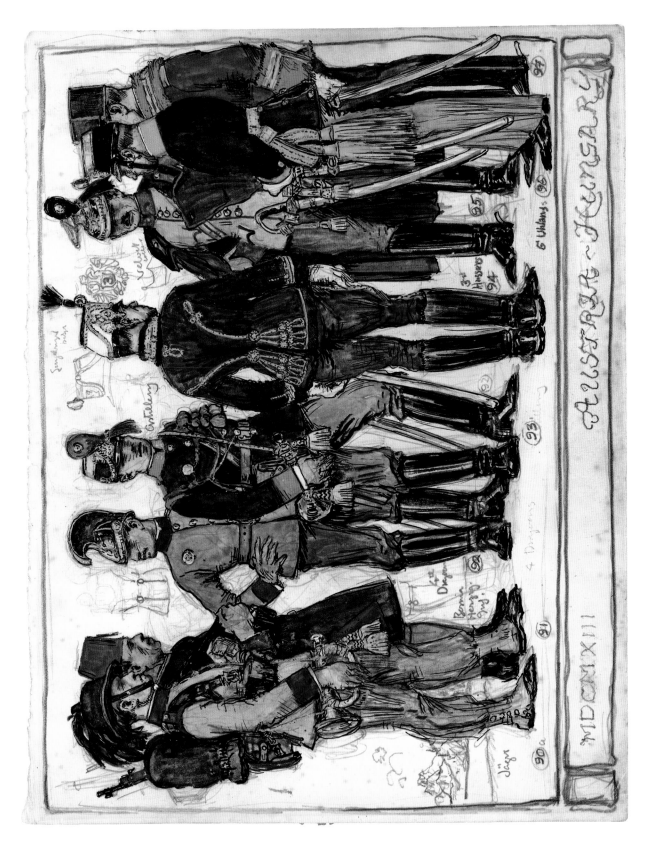

Plate 59

BELGIUM

Although 'Belgian' units fought at Waterloo, Belgium as a nation dates from 1830, when, not without some bloodshed, a Belgian kingdom and army were born. By 1910, when I first visited Belgium, it seemed to me that the soldier was almost more in evidence than in any other country – and very dress conscious. The army, although of course I knew little about it when making the drawings, consisted of Grenadiers, Infantry of the Line, *Chasseurs à Pied*, Carabiniers, Guides, *Chasseurs à Cheval*, Lancers, Horse, Field and Fortress Artillery, Engineers, Train (Army Service Corps) and Administrative Corps.

Although it is sixty-nine years since figure 1 was seen and drawn, it raises a very vivid memory of my first Belgian soldier, and of an unusually comforting feeling of well-being seated at a large window of what must have been the breakfast room of the most expensive hotel in Brussels. Something unaccustomed must have made my father, on arriving at the station (from Nuremburg it must have been), to cause him to feel a well-to-do British gentleman and finish our journey in style. My manner of life had been drastically changed during the previous week or two, following my parents coming to collect me at Munich. I can only suppose he had, as I do today, with a very short life possibility of the nineties, gone rather wild and decided that he had enough gold in his purse to last out the remaining days.

Items of particular note in the two Belgian plates are the so-called 'Tyrolean' hat, which was similar to that worn by the Austrian Tiroler Kaiserjäger, *and the forage cap with the minuscule peak, both of which were peculiar to the Carabinier Regiment (figures 1 and 8). The type of forage cap shown in figures 3, 6, 12, 13 and 18, known as a* bonnet de police, *first appeared in the French Army at the end of the eighteenth century. In the British Army, where it is called a 'tent hat', it is still worn by the officers of the Queen's Royal Hussars. Cap lines with flounders were worn by the Carabiniers and* Chasseurs à Pied *(pale yellow) and the Artillery (scarlet). For the officers of these units they were gold, and for the NCOs yellow or red mixed with gold.*

Various attempts were made to modernise the uniforms of the Belgian Army between 1911 and 1913, but, as Haswell Miller's drawings predate them, we are not shown any of them. In fact, they were not finalised when Belgium was invaded in 1914, and as a result the army went into action in a mixture of all possible uniforms, including full dress and 1913 trial items. It was not until December 1915 that a proper khaki service dress was introduced, stylistically a mixture of British and French influences, including the French Adrian steel helmet. (JM)

RANK BADGES

Staff officers

Colonel. *Vertical bar and three gold six-pointed stars on the collar.*

Lieutenant-Colonel. *Vertical bar and two gold six-pointed stars on the collar.*

Major. *Vertical bar and one gold six-pointed star on the collar.*

Subaltern officers

Captain. *Three gold six-pointed stars on the collar.*

Lieutenant. *Two gold six-pointed stars on the collar.*

Second Lieutenant. *One gold six-pointed star on the collar.*

Aspirant (Adjutant candidat-officier). *One silver six-pointed star on the collar.*

Non-commissioned officers

Warrant Officer (Adjutant). *One white or silver six-pointed star on the tunic and greatcoat collar. One row of narrow gold lace on the képi and scarlet piping on the side cap.*

Sergeant. *One or two gold or silver lace chevrons on both sleeves of the tunic and greatcoat.*

Corporal. *Two white or yellow inverted braid chevrons on both sleeves of the tunic and greatcoat.*

Private 1st Class. *One white or yellow inverted braid chevron on sleeves of the tunic and greatcoat. (JM)*

Plate 60: figures 1–10

Belgium, 1909.

1. Sergeant, Grenadier Regiment, parade dress, with two service chevrons on each arm.
2. Private, Carabiniers, service dress.
3. Trooper, 2nd Lancers, undress with forage cap.
4. Gunner, Artillery, service dress with forage cap.
5. Private, 1st *Chasseurs à Pied*, parade dress.
6. Trooper, 1st or 2nd Regiment of Guides, service dress with forage cap.
7. Trooper, 2nd Lancers, service dress. The lance pennant is in the Belgian national colours.
8. Private, Carabiniers, parade dress.

9. Private, Infantry of the Line, parade dress.
10. Private, Grenadier Regiment, undress.

Plate 61: figures 11–21

Belgium, 1910.
11. Lieutenant, 1st or 2nd Regiment of Guides, undress tunic and képi.
12. Lieutenant, 2nd *Chasseurs à Cheval*, undress.
13. NCO, 4th Lancers, undress with forage cap.
14. NCO, 3rd Lancers, parade dress.
15. Private 1st Class, 2nd *Chasseurs à Cheval*, drill order.
16. NCO, 2nd *Chasseurs à Cheval*, parade dress.
17. Gunner, Fortress Artillery, parade dress.
18. Trooper, 1st *Chasseurs à Cheval*, undress.
19. NCO, 2nd Regiment of Guides, parade dress.
20. NCO, Horse Artillery, parade dress.
21. NCO, 2nd *Chasseurs à Pied*, parade dress.

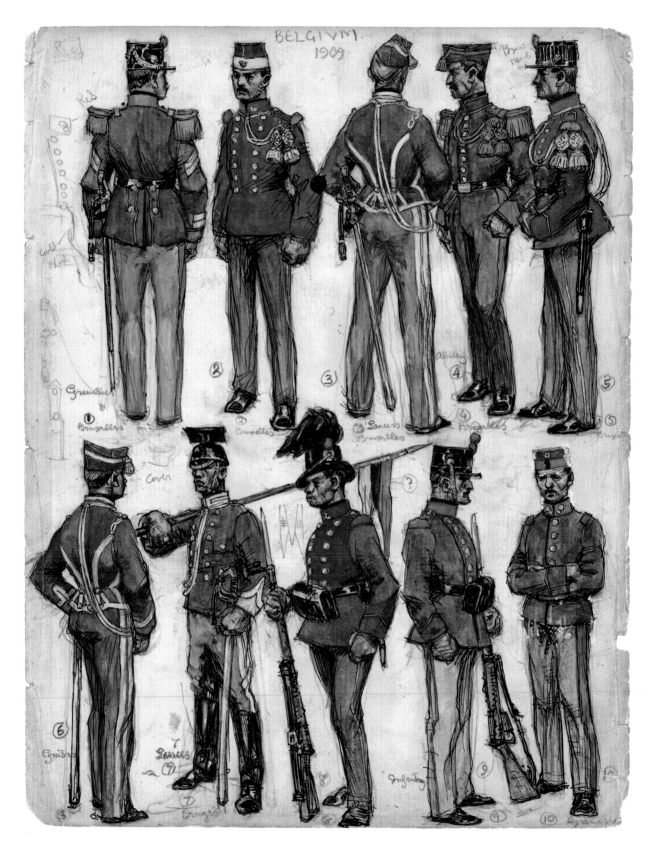

BELGIVM.
1909

Plate 60

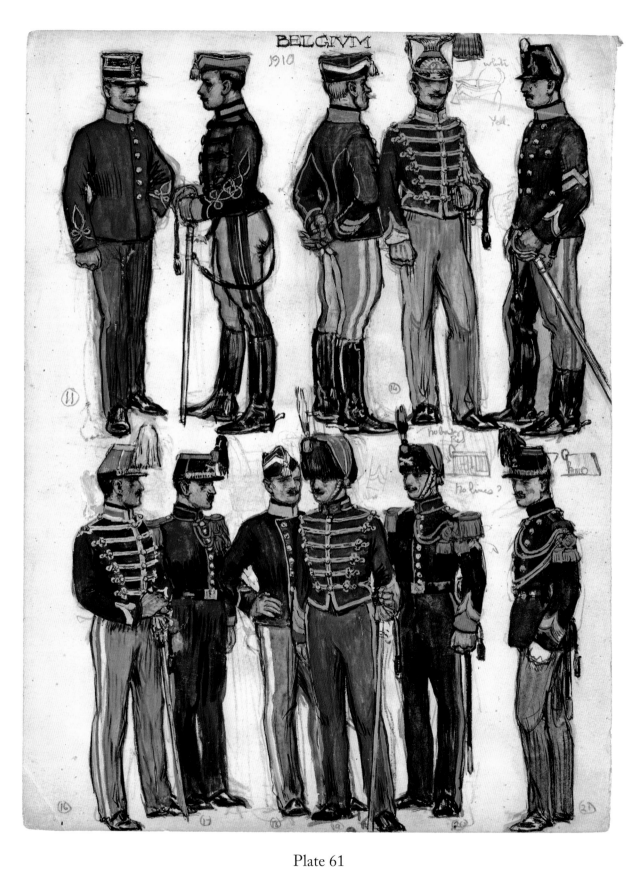

Plate 61

HOLLAND

Dutch uniforms before 1914 showed a mixture of influences, and had many variations. New uniforms were introduced in 1880, 1885, 1900, 1905 and 1912, both officers and men being allowed to wear their old uniforms until they wore out. As a result, some of the oldest patterns could still be seen in wear as late as 1909, when Haswell Miller was certainly in neighbouring Belgium. The majority of his figures are of dismounted troops, and the few mounted men have a rather British look, especially in their fur hussar caps and tunics; the NCOs' rank badges are similar to that of the French; and the musicians' 'swallow's nest' wings strike a Germanic note. Particularly Dutch features are the considerable use of the national colour orange as braid, and the variety of headdress. First of all there was the shako, similar in shape to its French counterpart, and dating back to the 1880s. Its cap lines, gold or silver cord for officers and red or yellow wool for NCOs and men, were worn unhooked and wound round the body, on occasions when other headdress was worn. There was also the képi, more like the Austrian undress shako than its French namesake, the low fur cap (*talpa*) worn by the Field and Fortress Artillery, the field service or forage cap (*veldmuts*) not unlike the British tent-cap, and the cavalry's hussar fur cap (*kolbak*).

In 1905 a single-breasted blue service dress tunic, or 'field coat' (*veldjas*), with breast pockets and the regimental number in red, on either the collar or the shoulder straps, was introduced for the infantry, to be used as an undress and for field service. At the same time the tall tent-cap was introduced. The former uniform was permitted to be worn for parades, although a new tenue was designed as a parade dress, as shown in figure 27. In 1912–13 a grey service dress with different arm-of-service coloured piping was introduced, which the Dutch Army wore when mobilised in 1914. The old blue uniforms continued to be worn into the 1920s.

RANK BADGES

Staff officers
Colonel. *Two gold lace bars and three stars in the button colour on the collar.*
Lieutenant-Colonel. *Two gold lace bars and two stars in the button colour on the collar.*

Major. *Two gold lace bars and one star in the button colour on the collar.*

Subaltern officers
Captain. *Three stars in the button colour on the collar.*
Lieutenant. *Two stars in the button colour on the collar.*
Second Lieutenant. *One star in the button colour on the collar.*

Non-commissioned officers
Sergeant-Major. *Two inverted chevrons of mixed wool (sometimes silk) and metal braid of the button colour above the cuff.*
Sergeant. *One inverted chevron of the braid of the button colour above the cuff.*
Corporal. *Two inverted chevrons of red or yellow wool braid above the cuff.*

Plate 62: figures 1–10

1. Officer Cadet (Guard *Jäger* Regiment), Royal Military Academy, parade dress. The white cap lines are worn attached to the shako.
2. Private, Engineers, walking-out dress with képi. The red cap lines are worn unattached.
3. Band Sergeant-Major, 7th Infantry Regiment, walking-out dress with the 1905 service dress tunic and képi.
4. Sergeant-Major, Royal Military Academy, service dress with képi.
5. Private, Grenadiers, parade dress. The white cap lines are worn attached to the shako.
6. Gunner, Field or Fortress Artillery, service dress.
7. Gunner, Horse Artillery, parade dress.
8. Trooper, 1st Hussars, stable dress with tent-cap.
9. Sergeant, infantry, walking-out dress with full dress tunic, képi and cloak. The single chevron on the upper arm is for ten years' service, and the small red stars are marksmanship badges.
10. Officer, Colonial Troops, service dress.

Plate 63: figures 11–20

11. Officer, possibly of the West Indies Service Corps, service dress with 1905 pattern tunic and képi.
12. Private, 4th Infantry, guard order with képi.

13. NCO, Field or Fortress Artillery, service dress and képi.
14. Private, Grenadiers, undress with the 1905 pattern tunic and képi.
15. NCO, Grenadiers, service dress with képi.
16. Gunner, Horse Artillery, service dress with tent-cap.
17. Back view of the same.
18. Major, 3rd Hussars, service dress.
19. Subaltern Officer, General Staff, service dress with képi.
20. Subaltern Officer, 1st Hussar Regiment, service dress.

Plate 64: figures 21–30

21. Lieutenant, Field or Fortress Artillery, undress with 1905 pattern tunic and forage cap.
22. Officer, Grenadiers, service dress with 1905 field tunic with képi.
23. NCO, Marines, service dress with képi.
24. Bandsman, 7th Infantry Regiment, with 1905 field tunic and képi.
25. Sergeant, KNIL (Royal Dutch East India Army), service dress with pre-1905 tunic and képi.

26. Sergeant, 7th Infantry, undress with 1905 field tunic with képi.
27. Private, 4th Infantry, service dress with 1905 new-style 'grand dress' tunic and képi.
28. Sergeant-Major, Field or Fortress Artillery, service dress with tent-cap.
29. Trooper, 1st, 2nd or 4th Hussars, undress with tent-cap.
30. Sergeant-Major, 3rd Hussars, service dress with képi.

Plate 65: figures 31–35

31. Lieutenant, 2nd KNIL Colonial Administration, service dress with képi.
32. Officer, General Staff, service dress with képi.
33. Second Lieutenant (Adjutant), Infantry, service dress with 1900 field tunic and képi.
34. Second Lieutenant, Engineers, walking-out dress with 1880 dress tunic and képi.
35. Second Lieutenant, *Jäger*, walking-out dress with 1880 dress tunic and képi.

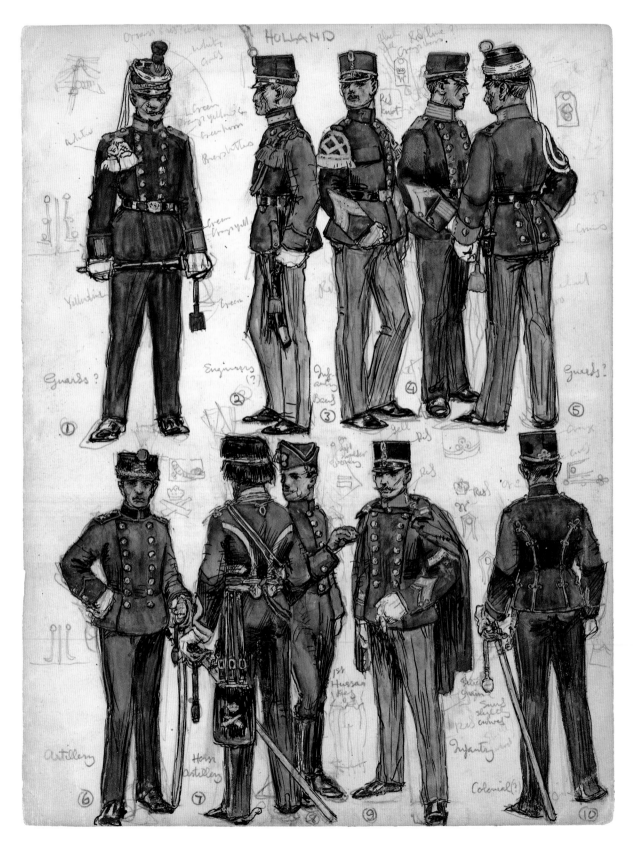

Plate 62

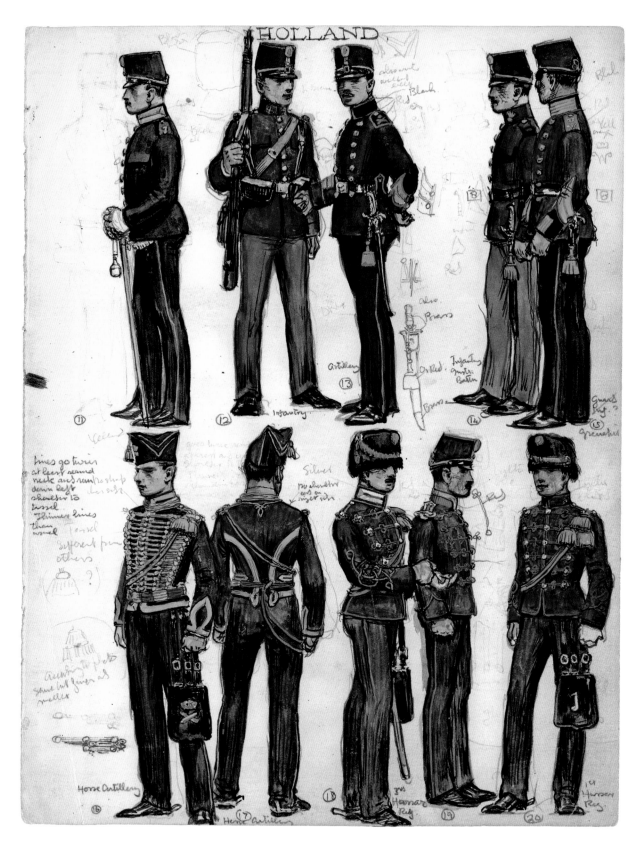

Plate 63

HOLLAND

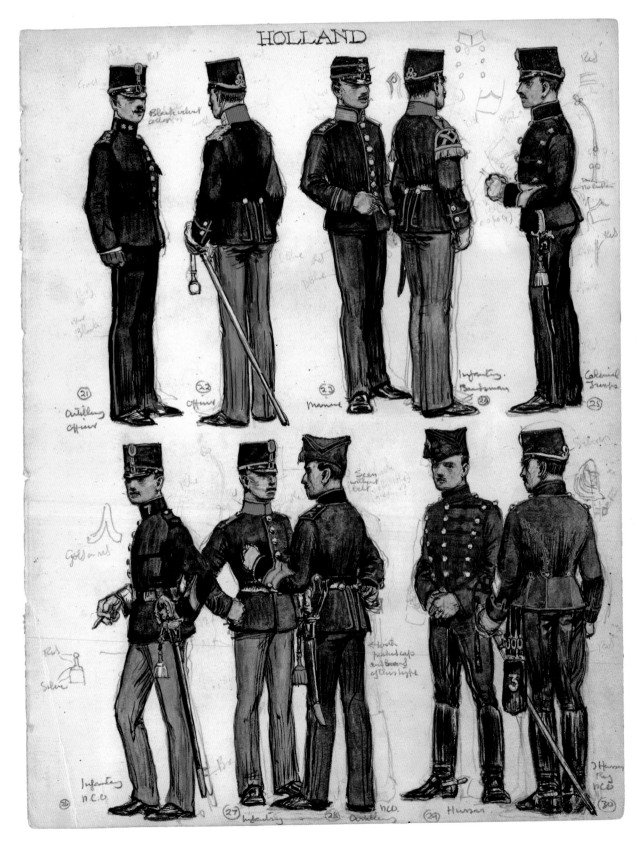

Plate 64

HOLLAND

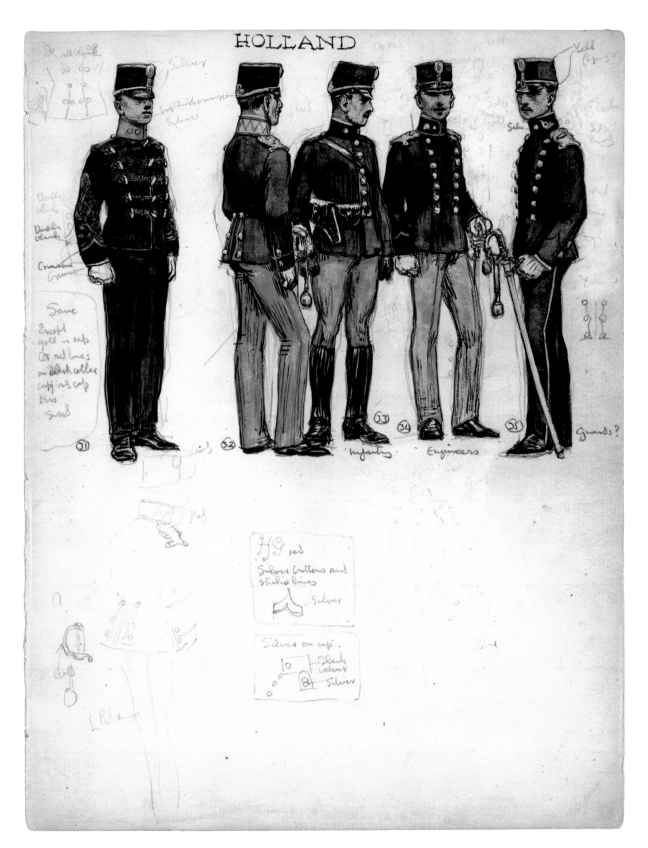

Infantry   Engineers

Plate 65

ITALY

The uniforms of the Italian Army, mainly blue with some French and Austrian influences, were virtually unchanged from 1873 to 1908, when a grey-green service dress was introduced. Between 1908 and 1915, when Italy entered the war, parts of the new grey-green uniform were worn with the old dark blue tunics. Haswell Miller shows several figures wearing this mixed dress in 1913.

Three Italian units which have caught the popular imagination and still exist are the Carabinieri, the Bersaglieri and the Alpini. The Carabinieri, still to be seen on the streets of Rome with their cocked hats and nineteenth-century tailed coats, were raised in 1814 to 'maintain public and private security'. In 1873, after Rome had been proclaimed the capital of the unified Italy, their headquarters were moved to Rome, and the 'King's Guard Carabinieri Squadron' was established. Dressed in metal helmets and cuirasses, this still provides the Italian Presidential Guard.

The Bersaglieri, formed in 1836 by General La Marmora, was originally a Sardinian regiment. They fought alongside the British and French during the Crimean War, and took part in the two wars of independence that culminated in the unification of Italy in 1861. Celebrated for their hats adorned with the cock feathers that they still attach to their steel helmets, and their running gait, the passo di corsa, they were an élite force of sharpshooters. A memento of the Anglo-Sardinian Crimean connection can be seen in the blue frogged and fur-trimmed pelisse, worn by figure 6, which was called a 'Spencer', the British name for a short outerwear jacket.

The Alpini, troops trained in mountain warfare and survival, with their distinctive bowler hat called the bombetta, were formed in 1872 to protect the mountainous borders of the recently unified Italy. Haswell Miller notes, in figures 1, 3 and 4, the curious arrangement, I think unique to the Italian army, whereby the tunics are slit at the sides up to the waist and secured by two buttons, allowing the belt, which is worn under the tunic, to pass through and appear in the front. (JM)

RANK BADGES

Until 1908 officers' rank badges consisted of one row of broad braid and one to three rows of narrow braid above the cuff, staff officers having only the broad braid. In addition staff and subaltern officers had from one to five rows of narrow braid round the base of the képi. After 1908 officers wore silver or gilt five-pointed stars on the shoulder straps of the patrol jackets, the blue service dress jacket and the greatcoat. It should be noted that the six-pointed stars worn on the collar by nearly every figure are not rank badges but the emblem of the Italian Army.

Although not visible in Haswell Miller's drawings, officers' rank was also shown on the metal epaulettes, those of staff officers being broader with bullion fringe and subalterns' narrower with plain fringe. The rank was further shown by the number of crescents stamped out on the metal of the epaulette strap above the fringe. (JM)

Staff officers
Colonel. Three stars and cord edging to the shoulder strap in the button colour.
Lieutenant-Colonel. Two stars and cord edging to the shoulder strap in the button colour.
Major. One star and cord edging to the shoulder strap in the button colour.

Subaltern officers
Captain. Three stars of the button colour on the shoulder strap.
Lieutenant. Two stars of the button colour on the shoulder strap.
Second Lieutenant. One star of the button colour on the shoulder strap.
Officer Cadet (Aspirante). One black star on the sleeve.

Non-commissioned officers
Senior Sergeant-Major (Maresciallo Maggiore). Three rows of cord of the button colour set lengthwise along the shoulder strap.
Sergeant-Major (Maresciallo Capo). Two rows of cord of the button colour set lengthwise along the shoulder strap.
Junior Sergeant-Major. One piece of cord of the button colour set lengthwise along the shoulder strap.
Staff Sergeant. One broad and two narrow gold or silver braid chevrons above the cuff.
Sergeant. One broad and one narrow gold or silver braid chevrons above the cuff.
Corporal. Two broad and two narrow red braid chevrons above the cuff.
Lance-Corporal. Two broad and one narrow red braid chevrons above the cuff.

Plate 66: figures 1–8, 1909

1. Private, Mountain Rifles (Alpini), service dress. Haswell Miller's first drawing of an Italian.

2. Sergeant, 10th Lancers (Vittorio Emanuele II), service dress.
3. Corporal, Engineers, parade dress.
4. Private, 80th Infantry Regiment (Rome Brigade), marching order.
5. Officer Cadet (First Year), service dress.
6. Field Officer, Engineers, winter service dress with pelisse, or 'Spencer'.
7. Lieutenant, Bersaglieri, service dress.
8. Private (one year), Engineers, most probably from the Military Academy of Turin, service dress.

Plate 67: figures 9–18, 1909

9. Trooper, Carabinieri, guard order.
10. Private, Sardinian Infantry, service dress.
11. Gunner, Artillery, drill order.
12. Private, Bersaglieri, drill or guard order.
13. Private, Infantry, winter marching order.
14. Gunner, Artillery, service dress.
15. Corporal, Frontier and Customs Police (*Guardia di Finanza*), service dress.
16. Trooper, Carabinieri, full dress.
17. Sergeant-Major (*Maresciallo*), Sardinian Grenadiers, service dress.
18. Lieutenant, 5th Lancers (Novara), service dress.

Plate 68: figures 19–28

19. Trooper, Carabinieri, service dress. Single stripe as for dismounted men with the short sword. Seen in Rome.
20. Lieutenant, 24th Light Cavalry (Vicenza), service dress with forage cap. Seen in Udine in 1909.
21. Lieutenant, Commissariat Department, service dress.
22. Lieutenant, 4th Infantry (Piedmont Brigade), full dress. The blue sash was also worn by officers on picket duty (Orderly Officers). The collar patches should be red.
23. Major-General, service dress.
24. Captain, 9th Lancers (Florence), service dress.
25. Lieutenant, Infantry, service dress.
26. Lieutenant, 16th Light Cavalry (Lucca), service dress with patrol jacket.
27. Private, Sardinian Grenadiers, service dress.
28. Trooper, Carabinieri Mounted Squadron, dismounted parade dress. Seen in Rome.

Plate 69: figures 29–38 (1913)

29. Sergeant, Engineers, service dress.

30. Trooper, 1st Line Cavalry (Nice), service dress with patrol jacket.
31. Lieutenant, 10th Lancers (Vittorio Emanuele II), mounted undress.
32. Lieutenant, Medical Corps, undress.
33. Lieutenant, 8th Lancers (Montebello), full dress.
34. Officer, Carabinieri, dismounted full dress.
35. Lieutenant, Engineers, full dress.
36. Lieutenant, Frontier and Customs Police (*Guardia di Finanza*), full dress.
37. Field-Officer, Artillery, full dress.
38. Lieutenant, 3rd Line Cavalry (Savoy), full dress.

Plate 70: figures 39–48 (1913)

39. Private, Engineers, service dress with blue tunic, 1908 grey-green forage cap and trousers, and black leather gaiters.
40. Gunner, Artillery, service dress with blue tunic, 1908 grey-green breeches and high black leather leggings.
41. Private, Infantry, marching order with 1908 pattern equipment.
42. Major, Medical Service, service dress with blue tunic.
43. Officer, Cavalry, service dress with blue patrol jacket.
44. Trooper, dismounted Carabinieri, service dress.
45. Private, Infantry, service dress with greatcoat.
46. Gunner, Artillery, service dress with peaked tent-cap.
47. Private, 55th or 56th Infantry Regiments of the Marche Brigade, guard order with greatcoat.
48. Trooper, 2nd Line Cavalry (Royal Piedmont), service dress with peaked tent-cap.

Plate 71: figures 49–58 (1913)

49. Trooper, dismounted Carabinieri, service dress with képi, blue tunic and grey breeches.
50. Corporal, Alpini, service dress with grey trousers and puttees.
51. NCO, 8th Lancers (Montebello), service dress.
52. Major, Sardinian Grenadiers, parade dress.
53. Captain, Carabinieri, service dress with blue patrol jacket and tent-cap.
54. Trooper, 21st Light Cavalry (Padua), service dress with grey breeches.
55. Corporal, Horse Artillery, dismounted parade dress.
56. Trooper, 17th Light Cavalry (Caserta), undress with 1908 grey-green [something missing] and trousers, and blue tunic.
57. Staff Sergeant, Horse Artillery, service dress.
58. Trooper, 4th Line Cavalry (Genoa), service dress.

Plate 66

ITALY 1909

Plate 67

ITALY

CAVALLEGG
-IERI
No 24
VICENZA

LANCIERI.
No 9
FIRENZE.

CAVALLEGGIERI
No 16
LUCCA.

Plate 68

Plate 69

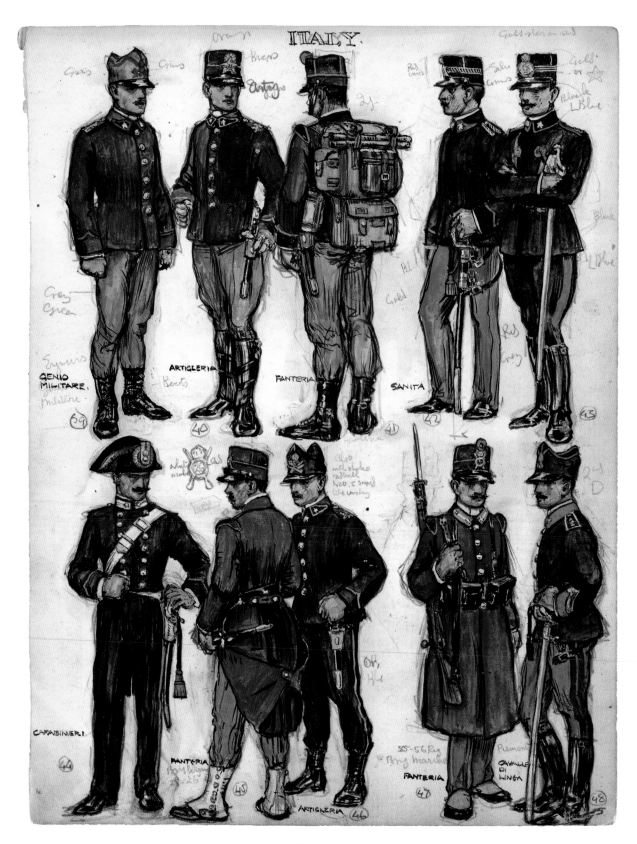

Plate 70

ITALY
1913

CARABINIERI.

ALPINI.

LANCIERI. N° 8

GRANATIERI. CARA-BINIERI.

CAVALLEGIERI. N° 21 PADOVA.

ARTIGLIERIA.

CAVALLEGIERI. N° 17 CASERTA.

ARTIGLIERIA.

CAVALLERIA DI LINEA N° 4. GENOVA.

Plate 71

PORTUGAL

Portugal entered the First World War in March 1916, and units sent to France were first trained and equipped in Britain. Their service dress was French horizon blue, but the cut of the uniforms was inspired by British models, their steel helmets being made in Birmingham. Although the uniforms of the three cavalry officers in this plate date back to 1900, the format and style of drawing are typical of Haswell Miller's post-war work. (JM)

Plate 72

Undated.

1. Cavalry, Second Lieutenant, service dress with peaked forage cap, back view.
2. Cavalry, Lieutenant, service dress with peaked forage cap, front view.
3. Cavalry, Lieutenant, service dress with blue undress tunic and with peaked forage cap.

PORTVGAL

Plate 72

RUSSIA

I can only say that I saw the ten officers that I have drawn. All were exceptionally professional and as soldierly as any I have ever seen. With the exception of figure 3, all were seen in London and must have been there either as embassy staff or officers on leave from the Russian Brigade or Division that appeared on the French Front about 1916 or 1917. It was hard to believe that these so competent looking soldiers were part of a great army that was to disappear in a matter of months.

The five figures that I have drawn are the only Russian soldiers I have ever seen, apart from Soviet officers who visited a prisoner of war camp in Lanarkshire where I was on the staff, during the Second World War. I am rather troubled about the central figure, who impressed me by his perfect and tasteful elegance and soldierly perfection. Since 1901 I have been sensible of the unique method of wearing the sword, reversed from the manner in which I have drawn it here. It may be that the officer, doubtless an attaché, had an alternative method officially permitted. When this sword was seen by me in 1901 and in photographs, during the following decades to the end of the Empire, it was usually slung from a narrow sword belt over the right shoulder outside the tunic, coat or jacket. In fact the method is the same as that surviving in the Scottish infantry regiments up to the present (or yester) day, and dates from the eighteenth century, for light infantry. I have been so careful with this sword I think I may be right, the sword belt being under the jacket. The officer was even, to my delight, just outside the Ministry in the Rue de Rivoli. I think it may have been the same day of the exciting apparition of the French sentry outside the Ministry of Marine.

The other four officers appeared to inspect an Irish Guards School of Instruction for NCOs (and Yeomanry Officers), to the staff of which I was appointed for a few months. I suppose I was little use for anything else, not being sent abroad until 1917. I think Sir Arthur Paget was the actual Inspector and I remember there was a well-known cricketer on his staff – name forgotten, but he was friendly to me. (Very class conscious then and there.) How I remember the 'Sah, may I introduce you to my wife' if, or when, the emergency of such an accidental encounter had to be dealt with. The Commandant, a nice Irish Guards Major, stood up to the horrors of having an HLI and a Royal Scot on his staff. I never felt he considered us quite human; a curious reserve made it absolutely unthinkable

that he should speak to more than one of us at a time if he had to unburden himself of the relation of some odd, amusing or scandalous occurrence.

Returning to the elegant Russians. Being winter, only one shed the more or less blue-grey greatcoat but I managed to see the Major-General's baggy trousers and the black and silver pantaloons and boots of the hussar officer. The Colonel, the left figure, was presumably wearing the uniform of the 2nd Regiment of a Division according to the light blue cap band. The 'Paris' captain's cap band denoted the 4th Regiment of a Division, and his service dress grey jacket had red piping around the collar and cuffs. The General's jacket was noted as plain, like figure 3, but without red piping. His breeches were of a bright 'Prussian' blue. He had a plain rather softer grey cap than the fourth (artillery) officer. His smart jacket had grey buttons and, oddly, was 'feminine'. It did not appear to have been so shabby as to have been remade – possibly it was a vanity, suggesting that the officer had suffered long and arduous service. (In the 1850s–70s this was often found in the British Army, evident in photographs of groups of officers.)

As Haswell Miller suspected, he got the suspension of the swords in figures 3 and 7 wrong. There was no upper suspension ring for the short sword sling, but a D ring loop on the inner side of the scabbard. The lower ring was in fact set on the front of the scabbard, not on the back as shown here.

The painful lessons learned by the Russian Army during the Russo-Japanese War of 1904–5 led to the universal adoption in 1906–7 of a khaki service dress, consisting of a peaked cap (furashka), linen shirt of traditional Russian shape (gimnasterka), and linen trousers tucked into boots for the summer, and for the winter, a fur cap (shapka), a woollen shirt and a greatcoat (shinel). Officers wore single-breasted khaki tunics with closed collars (kittel), linen in summer and cloth in winter. In 1913, to celebrate the tercentenary of the Romanov dynasty, numerous unpopular and clumsy embellishments were introduced to smarten up the khaki uniform as a substitute for full dress, but the outbreak of war brought this venture to an abrupt end.

In 1914 Russian officers favoured the 'English' look on service, and as a result started appearing in the long loose service dress jacket with huge pockets, known, perhaps as a compliment to the British Commander-in-Chief, Sir John French, as the 'French', or in some variant of the Norfolk jacket. However, perhaps because they were part of a diplomatic mission, the officers seen by Haswell Miller in London in 1917 had smartened themselves up, with the peacetime version of service dress, with coloured forage caps, gold or silver shoulder boards and dress breeches and trousers. When one considers that the Russian Revolution was about to break out, officers like this must have been a very rare sight. (JM)

RANK BADGES

As only officers appear in these plates, only officers' rank badges are given here. For some reason peculiar to Russia, full generals, colonels, and captains, the senior of each grade, had plain shoulder-boards without stars.

General. *Plain General's pattern zigzag lace of the button colour.*

Lieutenant-General. *The same with three five-pointed stars of the button colour.*

Major-General. *The same with two five-pointed stars of the button colour.*

Colonel. *Plain lace of the button colour with two narrow coloured stripes.*

Lieutenant-Colonel. *The same with three five-pointed stars of the button colour.*

Major. *The same with two five-pointed stars of the button colour.*

Captain. *Plain lace of the button colour with one narrow coloured stripe down the middle.*

Staff Captain. *The same with four five-pointed stars of the button colour.*

Lieutenant. *The same with three five-pointed stars of the button colour.*

Second Lieutenant. *The same with two five-pointed stars of the button colour.*

Ensign. *The same with one five-pointed star of the button colour.*

The colour of the lace, the double or single stripes and the material on which the lace was mounted depended on the unit or arm of service. Metal or embroidered badges as, for instance, crossed cannons for artillery regiments or the ciphers of Russian or foreign colonels of regiments, were added as required.

Although shoulder boards of khaki braid were introduced for wear with the khaki uniforms, Haswell Miller shows that the full-dress gold or silver lace versions were still being worn in 1917. (JM)

Plate 73: figures 1–5

1. Colonel of Infantry, service dress with coloured forage cap (2nd Regiment of a Division indicated by blue cap band) and greatcoat. London, 1916.
2. Major-General, service dress with greatcoat and dress breeches. Brentwood, 1917.
3. Captain, Life-Guard *Findlandski* Regiment, service dress with coloured forage cap (4th Regiment of the 2nd Guards Division indicated by green cap band). Three regimental badges on the left breast pocket. Paris, 1912.
4. Lieutenant of Artillery, service dress (with crossed cannon and three stars on shoulder board) and dress breeches. He wears the cross of the Order of St George (4th Class) on his left breast. The white patch on the right breast may have been intended for three separate academic badges, which were worn on that side. London, 1916.
5. Lieutenant, 5th Hussar Regiment, service dress (cipher of the Empress Alexandra Feodorovna and two stars on shoulder board) with coloured forage cap, dress breeches and greatcoat. Brentwood, 1917.

Plate 74: figures 6–10

6. Pilot (Captain), Aviation Service, service dress with Pilot's forage cap (*Pilotka*), dress breeches and boots.
7. Captain, 6th Gendarmes, undress with greatcoat.
8. Engineer Lieutenant, Imperial Navy, undress with greatcoat. The greatcoat should be black not dark blue, and the coloured lines on the shoulder boards black not red.
9. Lieutenant of Infantry, service dress with tunic/shirt (*gimnasterka*).
10. Lieutenant of Infantry (1st Regiment of a Division indicated by red cap band and red collar patch), undress with coloured forage cap and greatcoat.

Capt. Miller. 1917.

RVSSIA

(i) Infantry. Colonel. (2nd Regiment of a Division, indicated by blue capband.)

London 1916.

(ii) Major General. 2 stars on shoulder straps denoting rank. Plain tunic as (iii) but without red piping.

Brentwood 1917.

(iii) Infantry. Captain (4th Regt. of a Division, indicated by green capband.) Black sword knot with silver line at edge. Silver tassel with orange lines in ball. A gold eagle enamel on right breast pocket.

Paris 1912.

(iv.) Over-Lieutenant. Artillery. Crossed cannon and three stars on shoulder straps. Three s.s. seen with tunic as (iii). Order of St George worn.

(v) 5th Hussar Reg. "Alexandrija" (Empress Alexandra Fjodorowna) London 1916. (Ssamara) Lieutenant. Monogram ⟨AF⟩ and two stars on shoulder. Plain grey tunic.

Brentwood 1917.

Plate 73

RVSSIA

Plate 74

SPAIN

This section, not unnaturally perhaps, combines the memories of an old man living in, or even obsessed by, the past, and the magic of a childhood with the occasional appearance of a *Graphic*, bought as a mad extravagance by my father. Was it the celebration of the receipt of a good order? The *Graphic*: the memory is probably linked with the outbreak of the Spanish–American War of 1898, and one long-treasured issue of that weekly in which there were some drawings of Spanish uniforms. Somehow I already knew about the (now forgotten?) *Ros*, that unique headdress worn by the infantry and other dismounted units. The distortion of the cocked hat of the *Guardia Civil* was familiar through my unaccountable possession of an issue of a Spanish publication of the *Illustrated London News* type, of the 1870s, which contained an admirable painting of a *Guardia*. I was eventually to encounter them in 1914, rather unsatisfactorily since I was trapped in the heat of Seville by the outbreak of the 'Great War'. The *Ros* was never seen without its white cover, except in a hatter's shop in Sierpes.

My next visit to Spain was in 1920. The striped pyjamas were now supplanted by a greenish khaki, and *Ros* and *Guardia* hats were becoming elusive. Fifty years passed before I returned to Andalucia again. In a short space of a fortnight I must have seen perhaps a dozen soldiers, a larger proportion than in any other country, and one or two apparently taking pride in their somewhat inventive appearance.

The Guardia Civil, *a force of Gendarmerie not unlike the Italian* Carabinieri, *were, according to the* Navy and Army Illustrated *of 1898, 'familiar with the duty of suppressing popular outbursts'. The* Carabiniero *was a force of customs guards, over a thousand strong, organised into districts, paid and maintained by the Treasury.*

The Ros *cap, mentioned above, was peculiar to the Spanish Army and is best described as a stiff glengarry with a curving top and a peak. It is reputed to have been invented by a General Ros de Olano. It is interesting to note that the circular 'pill-box' cap, given up in the British Army in 1902, was still in use by both mounted and dismounted units of the Spanish Army after the war, but generally worn straight on the head, not tipped to one side in the British manner.*

In plate 76, Haswell Miller describes how he filled the gaps in his knowledge with items either seen on an actual soldier, or in a photograph, or hanging in a shop window. In figure 3 of the same plate he includes a horse for the first time, placing it behind the dismounted figures, in very much the same way as he did in his Imperial War Museum watercolours, which would suggest that this plate was drawn about 1920. Generally he leaves a lot of questions unanswered and it has not been possible to identify some of the figures because of their unfinished state. I have left his queries in the captions as he wrote them. (JM)

RANK BADGES

Staff officers
Colonel. *Three large eight-pointed stars on or above cuff.*
Lieutenant-Colonel. *Two large eight-pointed stars on or above cuff.*
Major. *One large eight-pointed star on or above cuff.*

Subaltern officers
Captain. *Three small six-pointed stars on or above cuff.*
Lieutenant. *Two small six-pointed stars on or above cuff.*
Second Lieutenant (Alferez). *One small six-pointed star on or above cuff.*

Non-commissioned officers
First Sergeant. *Three diagonal braids above the cuff in the button colour.*
Second Sergeant. *Two diagonal braids above the cuff in the button colour.*
Corporal (Cabo). *One diagonal braid above the cuff in the button colour.*

Plate 75: figures 1–5 (1914)

1. Sergeant, *Cazadores* (Rifles), summer service dress. Seen in Tangier.
2. Untitled, undress with blue winter tunic summer trousers and gaiters and pill-box cap. Seen in Seville.
3. Trooper, 16th Lancers, summer service dress. Seen in Granada.
4. Major, Horse Artillery, summer service dress. Seen in Seville.
5. Captain, 12th *Cazadores de Caballeria* (Mounted Rifles), service dress tunic, with summer breeches. This combination of uniform not seen but the tunic and cap seen in Granada at different times.

Plate 76: figures 1–5 (1914)

1. Private of *Cazadores*, guard order. The colour of equipment doubtful. Pattern and colour of trousers doubtful. Pattern and manner of wearing shoes doubtful. This is the only figure wearing the sandals, peculiar to the Spanish Army, known as *alpargatos*, considered the best footwear in hot and mountainous country.
2. Trooper, Mounted Rifles, winter service dress. Dolman as seen in Avila. Shako as seen in a shop in Madrid, but officers with silver lace on upper edge. Tunic as in figure 4. Breeches questionable. Possibly boots worn instead of leggings as shown.
3. Captain, *Guardia Civil*, summer service dress. Seen in Toledo. Browning pistol worn in front at waist (through slit). Double shoulder belt as in figure 4. Horse appointments very doubtful, also colour of GC on saddle bag.
4. Trooper, 4th Lancers, drill order. Seen in Burgos, with khaki tunic. Probable pattern of pouch belt with loop and hook for carbine.
5. Sergeant, Engineers, parade dress. Seen in Madrid. *Ros* shako as seen in a photograph. Questionable if belongs to Engineers. Tunic and sword as seen.

Plate 77: figures 6–11 (1921)

6. Officer Cadet, service dress.
7. Officer, Horse Artillery, parade dress.
8. Gunner, Horse Artillery, khaki service dress with *Ros* shako.
9. Private, *Guardia Civil*, service dress.
10. Officer of Cadet School (Instructor?), winter service dress with pelisse.
11. Trooper, 4th Lancers, undress with pill-box cap and khaki breeches.

Plate 78: figures 12–18 (1921)

12. Lieutenant, *Guardia Civil*, service dress.
13. Sergeant, *Carabiniero*, service dress.
14. Gunner, Artillery, parade dress. Also [*seen*] with thin piping at top of shako.
15. NCO, Guard Cavalry Regiment (?), service dress.
16. Trooper, Guard Cavalry Regiment, service dress.
17. Corporal, 27th or 28th Mounted Rifles, khaki service dress with pill-box cap.
18. Corporal, Artillery, service dress tunic, khaki breeches and leggings and pill-box cap.

Plate 79: figures 19–25 (1921)

19. Trooper, Artillery, khaki service dress with pill-box cap.
20. Sergeant, Mounted Rifles, khaki service dress.
21. Sergeant, 55th Infantry Regiment, service dress with khaki *Ros* shako.
22. Corporal, 50th Infantry Regiment, khaki service dress with *Ros* shako.
23. Officer, khaki service dress with dress sash and peaked cap.
24. Major, Guard Cavalry, service dress with peaked cap.
25. Sergeant, Colonial Infantry, khaki service dress with blue cummerbund and red fez.

Plate 80: figures 26–32 (1921)

Unfinished and untitled.
26. Corporal, Guard Cavalry (?), khaki service dress with peaked cap.
27. Private, *Guardia Civil*, guard order.
28. Private, *Guardia Civil*, guard order.
29. Second Lieutenant, *Guardia Civil*, parade dress.
30. Unidentified civilian. Haswell Miller gives no indication as to who this might be.
31. Private, Infantry, khaki service dress with *Ros* shako.
32. Private, *Guardia Civil*, service dress with pill-box cap.

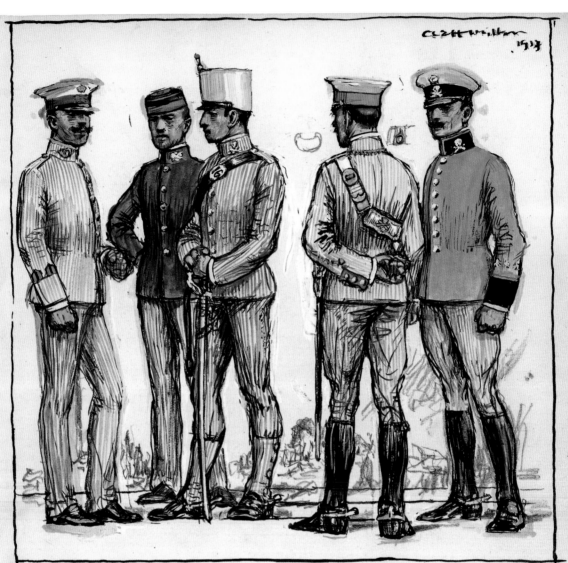

SPAIN. 1914

① Cazadores. (Rifles.) Summer uniform
Tangier

②

③ Cavalry 16th Regiment. Granada. Summer uniform
Seville

④ Artillery. Major. Summer uniform
Granada

⑤ Cavalry 16th Regiment. This combination of uniform not shorn
 and cap seen at different times.
Seville last time
Granada

Plate 75

SPAIN

CAZADOR

Colour of equipment
doubtful.
Pattern & colour of
trousers doubtful.
Pattern and mode
of wearing shoes
doubtful.

CAVALRY.

Dolman as seen in
AVILA. Chako as
seen in shop in MADRID
but officers with silver
lace on upper edge.
Tunic as in ④
Breeches questionable?
Possibly boots worn in-
stead of leggings as
shown.

CIVIL GUARDS.

As seen in TOLEDO.
Browning pistol
worn in front at
waist (though slit)
Double shoulder belt
as in ④
Horse appointments
very doubtful. Also colour of
S.C on saddle bag

CAVALRY
(CABALLERIA. LANCEROS
DE BORBON)
BURGOS
Seen with khaki
tunic.
Probable pattern of
pouch belt with
loop and hook for
carbine?

ENGINEERS

(ROS)
Chako as
seen in photo
? if belongs to
Engineers.
Tunic and
sword seen in
MADRID
? Trousers.

Plate 76

SPAIN 1921

⑥ Cadet.

⑦ Artillery.
Officer.

⑧ Artillery

⑨

⑩ Guardia Civil

Officer of Cadet School

⑪ Cavalry.

Plate 77

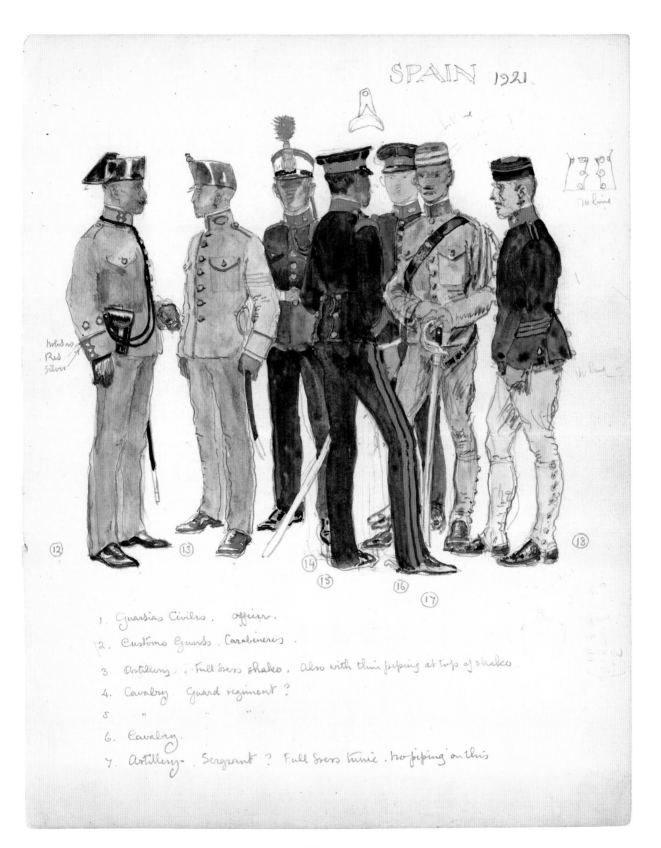

SPAIN 1921.

twists as
Red
Silver

76 line

⑫ ⑬ ⑭ ⑮ ⑯ ⑰ ⑱

1. Guardias Civiles. Officer.

2. Customs Guards. Carabineres.

3. Artillery. Full dress shako. Also with thin piping at top of shako.

4. Cavalry Guard regiment ?

5.   "   "   "

6. Cavalry.

7. Artillery. Sergeant ? Full dress tunic. no piping on this

Plate 78

SPAIN 1921

Plate 79

SPAIN 1921

Plate 80

SWEDEN

Haswell Miller left no explanatory note to account for this single plate of Swedish infantry uniforms, other than, in seven cases, the name of the regiment and the fact that he saw them in Sodra Skanska. The other two he saw during his stay in Munich. The general feel of these uniforms is Austrian and they are not dissimilar to the uniforms worn by the Royal Guards in Stockholm today. Like Spain, Sweden was neutral during the First World War. (JM)

Plate 81: figures 1–9

1. Officer, Infantry Regiment No. 25, service dress. Seen in Sodra Skanska, 1911.
2. Private, Infantry Regiment No. 25, service dress. Seen in Sodra Skanska, 1911.
3. NCO, Infantry Regiment No. 25, service dress. Seen in Sodra Skanska, 1911.
4. NCO, Infantry Regiment No. 25, service dress. Seen in Sodra Skanska, 1911.
5. Officer, Infantry, service dress with greatcoat. Seen in Munich, Türkenstrasse, 1909.
6. Back view of the figure 5.
7. Back view of figure 1.
8. Back view of figure 3.
9. Front view of figure 4.

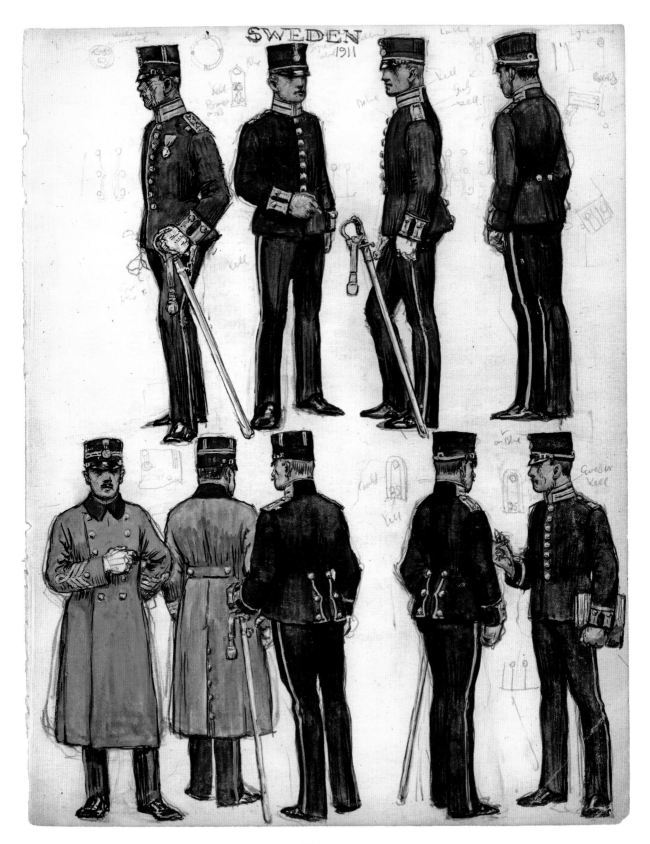

SWEDEN
1911

Plate 81

SELECT BIBLIOGRAPHY

Allmayer-Beck, J. C., and Lessing, E. *Die K. (u.) K.-Armee 1848–1914.* Prisma Verlag, Vienna, 1980.

Barthorp, M. J. *British Infantry Uniforms since 1660.* Blandford, Poole, 1982.

Barthorp, M. J. *British Cavalry Uniforms since 1660.* Blandford, Poole, 1984.

Barthorp, M. J. *The Old Contemptibles.* Osprey, London, 1989.

Bueno, J. M. *El Ejercito de Alfonso XIII, Tropas de la Casa Real.* Ediciones Barreira, Madrid, 1982.

Bueno, J. M. *El Ejercito de Alfonso XIII, Los Cazadores de Caballeria.* Ediciones Barreira, Madrid, 1983.

Carman, W. Y. *British Military Uniform.* Arco Publishing, London, 1957.

Cart, A. *Uniformes des régiments français de Louis XV à nos jours.* Éditions Militaires Illustrées, Paris, 1945.

Fosten, D. S. V. *Dress Uniforms of the Imperial German Cavalry 1900–1914, Cuirassiers and Heavy Cavalry.* Almark, New Malden, 1973.

Hagger, D. H. *Uniforms of the Imperial German Cavalry 1900–1914, Hussars and Mounted Rifles.* Almark, New Malden, 1973.

Hepke, Colonel. *Die Heere und Flotten – France.* Berlin, 1900.

Knötel, H., and Sieg, H. *Handbuch der Uniformkunde.* Verlag Diepenbroick-Grüter & Schulz, Hamburg, 1937.

Mollo, A. *Army Uniforms of World War I.* Blandford, Poole, 1977.

Mollo, B. *Uniforms of the Imperial Russian Army.* Blandford, Poole, 1979.

Mollo, E. *Russian Military Swords, 1801–1917.* Historical Research Unit, London, 1969.

Mollo, J. *Military Fashion.* Barrie & Jenkins, London, 1972.

Schenk, Colonel V. K. *The Tables of Uniforms of the Imperial Russian Army.* St Petersburg, 1911.

Woodward, D. *Armies of the World 1854–1914.* Sidgwick & Jackson, London, 1978.

Dress Regulations for the Army. London, 1911.

Gazette des uniformes.

Military Illustrated – Past and Present.

The Navy and Army Illustrated.

Tradition Magazine – Uniformes et Figurines.

Uniformes – Les Armées de l'histoire.

THE ARMY MUSEUMS OGILBY TRUST

(Registered Charity no. 250907)

The Trust (AMOT) is a registered charity founded in 1954 by the late Colonel Robert Ogilby DSO, DL, whose personal experiences in two world wars persuaded him that the fighting spirit of the British soldier stemmed from the *esprit de corps* fostered by the Army's regimental structure. This spirit is enshrined in the many regimental and corps museums across the United Kingdom, which seek to inspire and educate their visitors. Details of all these museums, advice on researching Army ancestors, and more about the Trust itself can be found on its website at www.armymuseums.org.uk.

The British Army has a rich history that is added to continually as today's regiments carry forward the proud traditions of their forebears. Their museums record this history, linking the past to the present, for the benefit of posterity. The Trust assists such museums with funds, advocacy, information and advice. Its income is derived solely from donations and bequests, and it would warmly welcome gifts, legacies or covenants from those who share its pride in our military heritage and its belief in the value of bringing it to the attention of the public.

Please help the Trust by:

Making a Donation

However small, a donation for help to fund the Trust's activities would be most gratefully received by the Director at:

The Army Museums Ogilby Trust
58 The Close,
Salisbury
Wiltshire SP1 2EX

Considering a Legacy?

Further information and a suitable form of words are available on our website at:

www.armymuseums.org.uk

Your generosity could have a profound impact on the preservation of the Nation's military heritage.

INDEX